Contents

п1 **The New Pygmalion**
Michael Paraskos

п2 **To carve is to love**
Sarah Davis

п3 **Tradition in stonecarving: use it or lose it**
Tim Crawley

п4 **Is this carving? Towards a definition of carving**
Matthew Rowe

п5 **Learning to read the cuts: why we need to copy historical ornamental woodcarvings**
Takako Jin

п6 **Why hand carving still matters in the 21st century**
ChatGTP

п7 **To survive, does carving need a Dada moment?**
Michael Paraskos

п8 **Musings from a restoration stone carver**
Akira Inman

п9 **Where is our real guild? Carvers, co-operativism and the guild ideal**
Charles Tomlinson

пX **Sophrosyne: Profile of Ekkehard Altenburger**
Michael Paraskos

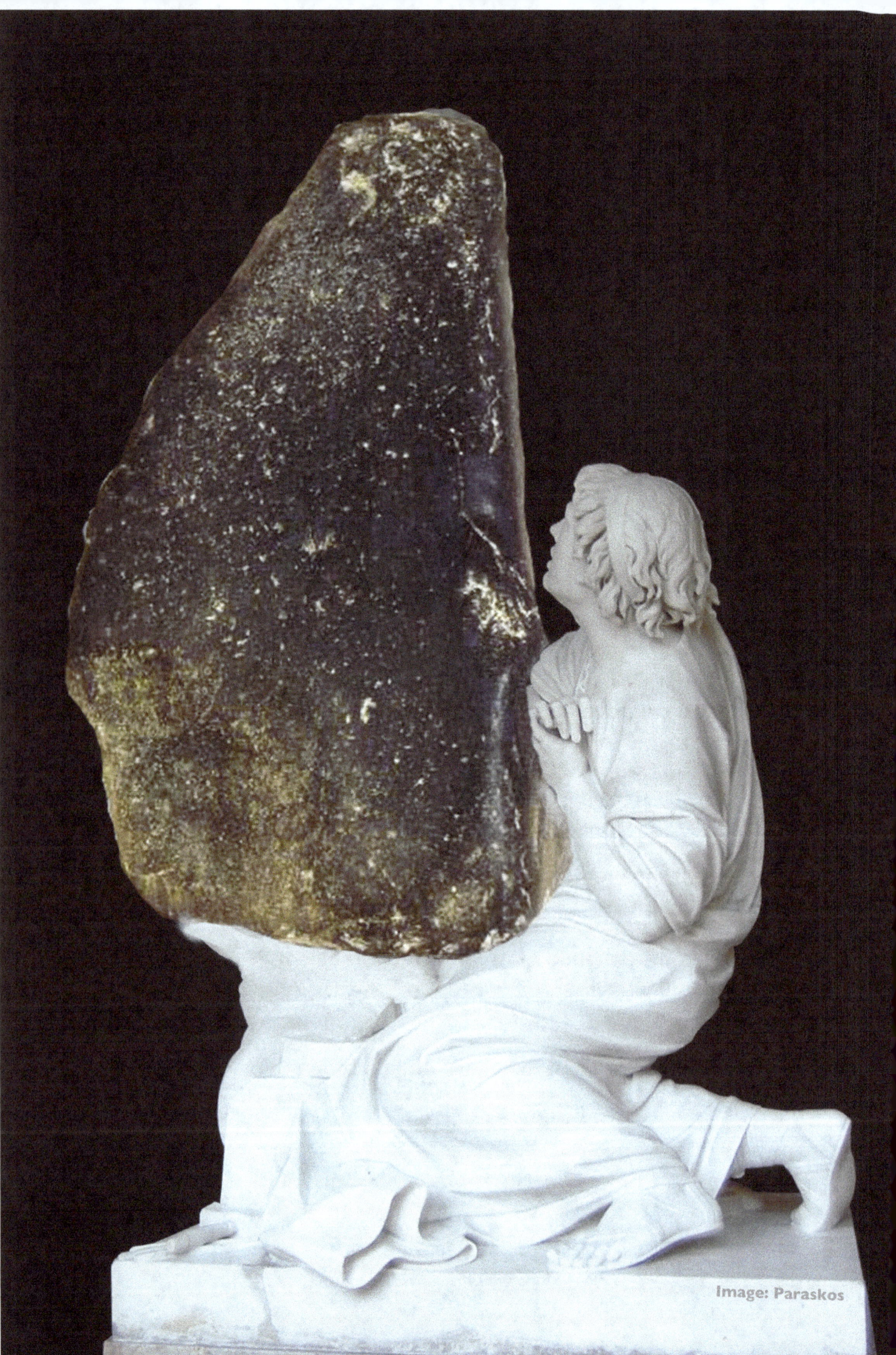

∏1 PROVOCATION 1

The New Pygmalion by Michael Paraskos

In 1954, the poet and art critic Herbert Read published one of his most interesting political books, *Anarchy and Order.* Even in his political writings, Read never strayed too far from art, believing art to be central to society, and therefore important politically. This can be seen in the introduction to *Anarchy and Order* where Read wrote: 'Society exists to transcend itself, and the progressive force of its evolution is the poetic imagination'. This was intended as a revolutionary statement — a belief that society must evolve, or transcend its existing form, and the engine for this revolutionary transcendence is art. But Read's conception of revolution meant more than just replacing all those mean and nasty managers of capitalist banks, factories and universities with kind and friendly socialist managers. A simple replacement of one group of people with another group of (supposedly nicer) people would have seemed to him a rather mundane form of revolution. To be worthy of the name, revolution would need to lead to a kind of psychological, or even spiritual, transcendence, resulting in 'new fields of consciousness' opening up to humanity.

As Read was one of the leading writers on the work of several key carvers in the twentieth century, I hope his writing will interest carvers today. I do not just mean in terms of his specific work on carvers like Barbara Hepworth and Henry Moore, but in the importance he set in embracing the political import of art, including the art and craft of carving. Read was, in many respects, an heir to the thinking about the arts and crafts embodied in the socialist and anarchist beliefs of William Morris, Walter Crane and William Lethaby, for all of whom the activities of carvers and other craftspeople should not give comfort to the wealthy beneficiaries of existing society. It should challenge their very existence by positing possible new ways of life and new modes of thinking. To justify its continued existence, carving should, along with the other creative arts and crafts, challenge the nature of reality itself, perhaps even following the line of Read's contemporary, Francesco de Sanctis, who wrote:

> When a subject comes into the brain of a creative writer, it at once dissolves that part of reality which suggested it. The earthly images seem to fluctuate, like objects in a mass of vapour seen from above. The figures — the trees, the towers, the houses — disintegrate, becoming fragmentary. To create reality, a poet must first have the force to kill it.

What an extraordinary claim. The artist exists to create a new reality, but in order to create that new reality the artist must kill the old one. Not just an extraordinary claim, but a revolutionary one, so different from the cosying up, so often seen in the crafts movement today, to the very people responsible for the destruction of craftsmanship.

At a time when hand carving seems so often under threat, I want to follow this line of thinking, and in particular Read's ideas, to suggest a possible reason for carving's continued existence as a relevant human practice, now and well into the future.

At the heart of Read's understanding of carving, at least in relation to Henry Moore, was the connection between the carver and physical reality. First and foremost in this was the earth, not only in terms of the chunk of earth being carved — the rock or wood that has come from the earth — but the earth into which the carver was born, grew up and lives. In Moore's case Read placed an emphasis on what he saw as Moore's kinship with his native landscape of Yorkshire, although that word, landscape, has to be taken broadly.

Writing in 1965, Read noted Moore's family were coal miners, giving them a long history of working with the rocky ground, but he also flagged up Moore's childhood reminiscences of playing in the natural world that surrounded him. Read described the sculptor's childhood as a time spent roaming 'the lanes and footpaths, bird nesting or gathering wild flowers.' Out of this experience a relationship developed between Moore and the rocks and nature of Yorkshire that would underpin Moore's art for the rest of his life. Remarkably, however, Read describes this as a familial relationship, one he called *kinship*. Moore was 'kin to the stone' of Yorkshire.

It was not just Moore who had this relationship. In his autobiography, *The Contrary Experience*, Read emphasised his own kinship towards the stones and earth of the Yorkshire landscape. For Read this was an ancient landscape 'pocked with small quarries from which people have taken the stone to build their houses and churches' for centuries. Again, his own longstanding familial connection to the Yorkshire landscape and his childhood experiences of playing in it were paramount. Read wrote that his own relationship began with:

> the stone flags of the kitchen floor and the passages of my house... they extend to the external walls, abraded by rain and frost, sun-soaked and annealed to the hill behind the house. Each step in the garden, and beyond the macadamised scar of the public road, is like the shift of a slide in some magic lantern, revealing a new pattern of stones or grasses, of bark or leaves, bushes and gateposts, cart-tracks and hedges, till finally the eye lifts to the explosive splendour of the oaks and ashes, the beeches and elms.

It is easy to recognise here an organic integration of the different elements being described, the human, the ancient dwelling, the stones, the plants and so on, forming a holistic entity. Within that context, it is as if each has become an aware being, each with its own sense of independent existence, but together forming an integrated and harmonious structure. Only the tar-macked road is presented as an unwelcome intrusion into this inscape, described by Read as a 'scar'. Read appears to see this integrated structure as something that is part physical, part psychological and part artistic, or poetical. Of course, it is important to remember that Read was also an artist, a poet, and so this landscape was just as important to him in his own creative work as it was to Moore in his. It is as though not only the perceiving human mind, but the stones of the houses, the rocks and plants of nature and the life of the surrounding landscape all have a kind of unique internal life on which the artist, carver or poet, draws for inspiration. While this is not the same as saying the stones and plants are sentient, they do seem to have what is today referred to by cultural theorists as agency, which is to say that while they are are connected to human consciousness, they also have an independent existence of their own, separate from the human gaze perceiving them, and that existence has its own, non-human, value. In Read's work this quasi-sentience (or perhaps non-human sentience is a better word) seems at times to pass into the resulting work of art, as we shall see in relation to the sculptural elements in Read's 1935 novel *The Green Child*.

Even if we are unwilling to accept actual non-human sentience, the concept of quasi-sentience can be useful in de-centring ourselves in our engagement with nature. Nature does not exist for the human gaze, or human entertainment, and by positing natural forms as having at least their own existence, or an agency that has nothing to do with the human, we recognise that we are not the centre of all things. In this we might even see a fundamental different between a discourse that is carving and a discourse that is fine art, in which the egotism of the fine artist is replaced by the modesty of the carver in the face of nature. While the fine artist might want to impose their will on materials, to illustrate their, no doubt very important, ideas, thoughts, beliefs and feelings, like a patriarch imposing its will on the world, the carver might want to ask whether they have a right to carve the block of stone or wood in front of them at all, or even if the stone or wood wants to be carved.

In saying this I really do risk suggesting objects are sentient, which sounds ridiculous. How can a block of stone or wood be sentient? Yet Read too, surprisingly frequently, came close to suggesting exactly this. One of the most striking examples is in *The Green Child*, in which a Read-like character, called Oliver, encounters what can only be described as sentient Henry Moore sculptures, each with green skin resembling Hornton stone, and facial features taken directly from Moore's figure carvings of the 1930s. In *The Green Child* the living Moore carvings inhabit a subterranean world and they not only have consciousness and agency, but they help Oliver to achieve a state of transcendence over his old understanding of reality. In other words, a revolution in Oliver's psychology takes place, and a new state of consciousness is achieved.

Read was even more explicit in suggesting the sentience of seemingly inanimate sculpture a short time later, when he performed a prose monologue at the opening of the 1936 International Surrealist Exhibition, held in London. In keeping with the Dada-esque quality of this event, Read delivered his monologue, entitled *The Surrealist Object*, whilst bouncing up-up-down on a bed, as though on a trampoline. The monologue itself was spoken not in Read's voice, but as though delivered by a sculpture, or a Surrealist object, which declared:

> This is the Surrealist object speaking to the British public. It has become necessary for the objects to explain themselves to the people. For convenience, I speak on behalf of other objects.

But this was not the first time Read had written on sculptures having autonomy from those who created or viewed them. Reviewing Jean Cocteau's often disturbing, film, *The Poet's Blood* in 1930, which again includes talking sculptures, Read wrote that the mechanism to make such a flight of fancy possible was that the talking sculpture appeared in a work of art, and as such it existed in a transcendent artistic time and space, emancipated from the restrictions placed on ordinary reality, a fact that might need further consideration.

All of this appears to create a paradox. On the one hand we have Read talking about art, and particularly the art of carving, as being born from a close and deep personal relationship between carver and their environment. This appears to be a kind of ego-topography in which the artist remains central, operating as a kind of nexus for the disparate elements of nature being focussed into the work of art. And on the other hand Read appears to suggest that both natural and art objects have a kind of sentient self-identity, or at the very least their own agency which is distinct from that of the artist and may, at times, be antithetical to the artist.

It is tempting to resolve this paradox with the commonplace notion that there are profound inconsistencies in Read's thought — and it is true, Read did change his mind quite often as an art theorist. But I think that is a mundane and ploddingly pedestrian way to try and understand Read. More compelling is the realisation that Read was grappling towards a difficult and revolutionary understanding of *the nature of being* that sought not divide the world into human sentient subjects and non-human insentient objects, but somehow to unite the two. This radical ontology can be seen as a hestitant move by Read towards reconceptualising the nature of being as a holistic interaction with the world in which the binary categories of subject (human) and object (non-human) break down. I do not think Read completed this move, but what he points towards is a radical egalitarian ontology that would have been consistent with his political views as an anarchist. The posssession of beingness and agency brings with it certain practical rights, including the right to decide for oneself and the right to some protections under law. What I think Read forces us to consider through his examples of walking-talking-sculptures, and the concept of being *kin to the stone*, is whether a far more distributed concept of agency and beingness can feature in how we engage as carvers and other makers with the world around us. He challenges us to see existence as a kind of interconnected matrix in which we should operate as matrixial partners with the rest of reality, rather than patriachal overlords imposing our form on it.

Read has not been alone in this, and I suspect in his own time the seeds for his thinking came from Bergson's concept of the interpenetration of nature embodied in the term the *élan vital*, and Alfred North Whitehead's ideas around interconnetedness. Later Merleau-Ponty, also argued that the human experience of the world is not based on active human beings perceiving passive non-human

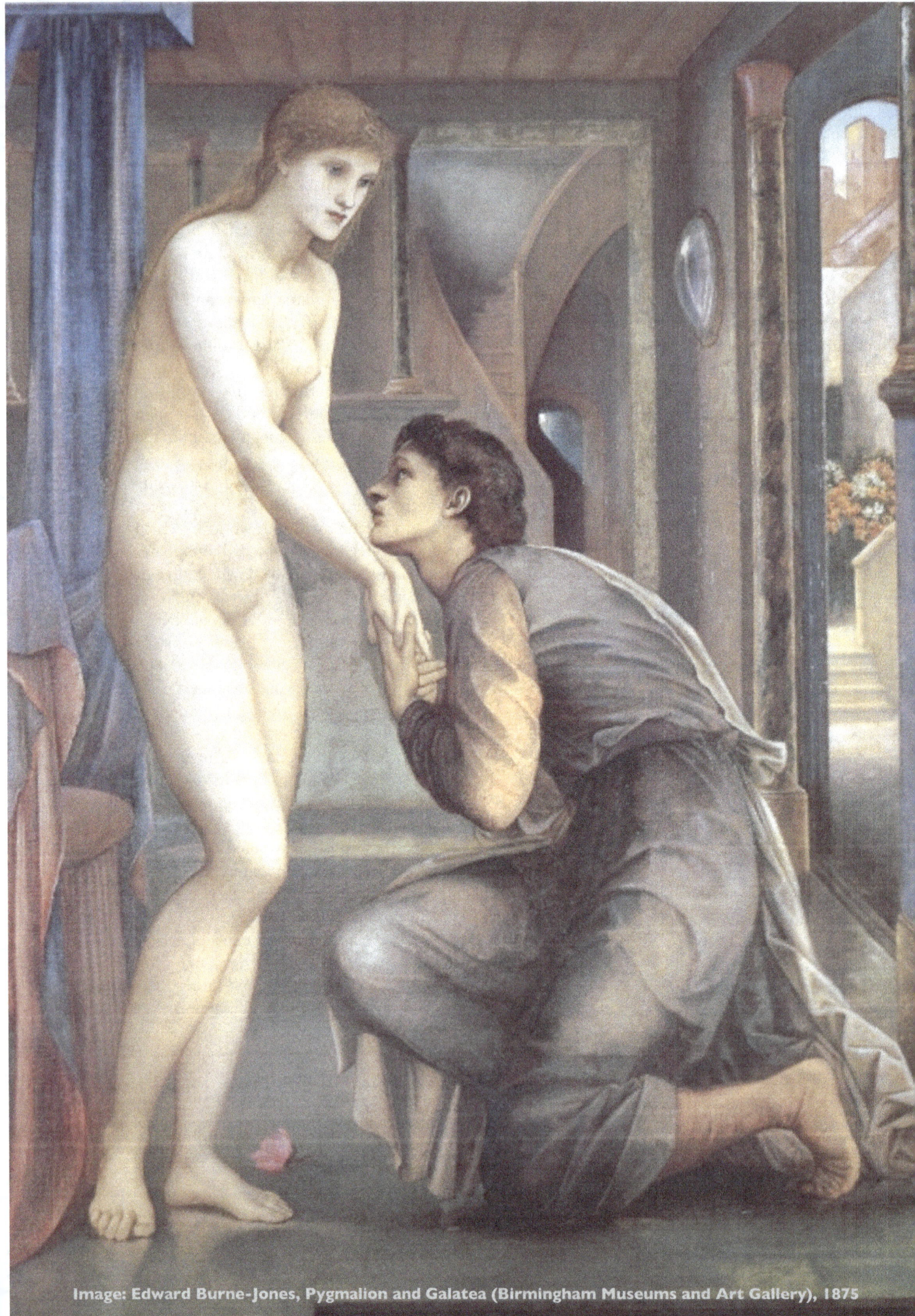

Image: Edward Burne-Jones, Pygmalion and Galatea (Birmingham Museums and Art Gallery), 1875

things, but on a dynamic engagement in which existences intertwine. Jane Bennett's reading of Gilles Deleuze, in her 2010 book *Vibrant Matter*, also springs to mind, with Bennett extending a concept of agency to non-human things through the idea of the 'agency of assemblages' in which agency is not the attribute of an individual conscious body, but 'depends on the collaboration, cooperation, or interactive interference of many bodies and forces'. Particularly important for me in recent months has been my discovery of the writings of the artist Bracha Ettinger, who characterises the interconnectedness as a kind of matrixial space of organic relationships, in profound opposition to a patriarchal space of differences.

For some it will seem too far fetched to talk of stone and wood having agency, let alone sentience, and perhaps it is. But I wonder how many carvers reading this have had the experience of seeming to be directed to carve, from cut to cut, not by a conscious voice in their heads, but seemingly from the stone or wood itself, as if it was directing where to place the hammer and chisel. I know I have experienced a parallel phenomenon in writing, when it is not clear who is writing, me or the text itself. At times like that, a kind of joy is experienced in the creative act, and from a carving point of view, I would have thought forcing a form onto a block of stone or wood, as if it is the powerless recipient of ominously phallic chisel blows, is a disturbing experience. Surely far better the block be a willing partner.

But I digress. To return to my point, there is clearly a longstanding interest in the development of radical ideas on *the nature of being* as a critical theory that is relevant to carvers. Through Read, and others, those ideas have the potential to offer a viable justification for carving in the twenty-first century, beyond trying to persuade people to like carving because it is ancient, lovely and skillful. Many things are ancient, lovely and skillful, but to survive a far better philosophical justification is needed, and I believe that in the ideas of Read and others there appears to be the potential for something truly extraordinary and fundamental. If carving is to survive it is up to carvers to engage with these ideas as they are the true weapons in our fight.

As Kenneth Gross suggested in his 1992 book, *The Dream of the Moving Statue*, there is a long history of viewing carvings and other sculptures as sentient, from Ovid's retelling of the Greek myth of Pygmalion, to Shakespeare's *A Winter's Tale*. It is there too in Molière's *Dom Juan*, Pushkin's *The Bronze Horseman*, Meyrink's *Der Golem*, and Oscar Wilde's *The Happy Prince*. Gross speculates that we might even have a psychological need to see in the apparently passive and dead something that is active and alive, motivated by a primal desire to recover the lost voices 'from the marble of art and the silence of history'.

Breaking the barrier between the quick and the dead is a theme that has haunted the human imagination since our earliest ancestors huddled against the dark around their makeshift camp fires, right through to the monuments to modern religion. In all that time art, especially the art of carving, has been seen as a central element to break that barrier. It makes me wonder whether there is something in the physical relationship between the carver and the wood or stone that he or she works that has a unique capacity to give visual voice to things that we ordinarily choose to see as dead and mute.

But perhaps I have gone too far. Living rocks and water, and the enfranchisement of plants and animals, might be too much to bear. Perhaps I should follow Read's example and be more wary when I whisper such things to modern ears. But, even if Read was not explicit, I believe there is plenty of circumstantial evidence to show that he was grappling towards these ideas when he gave voice to the Henry Moore sculptures in *The Green Child*, made a Surrealist object speak, and when he saw himself as kin to the stone. By rejecting the patriarchal division between subject and object Read can be seen as attempting to formulate a radical new reality, a new ontology, which would transcend existing object relationships by viewing existence, not as a division between the powerful and the powerless, but as a complex interplay between diverse and equally empowered actors, whether human, animal, mineral or vegetable.

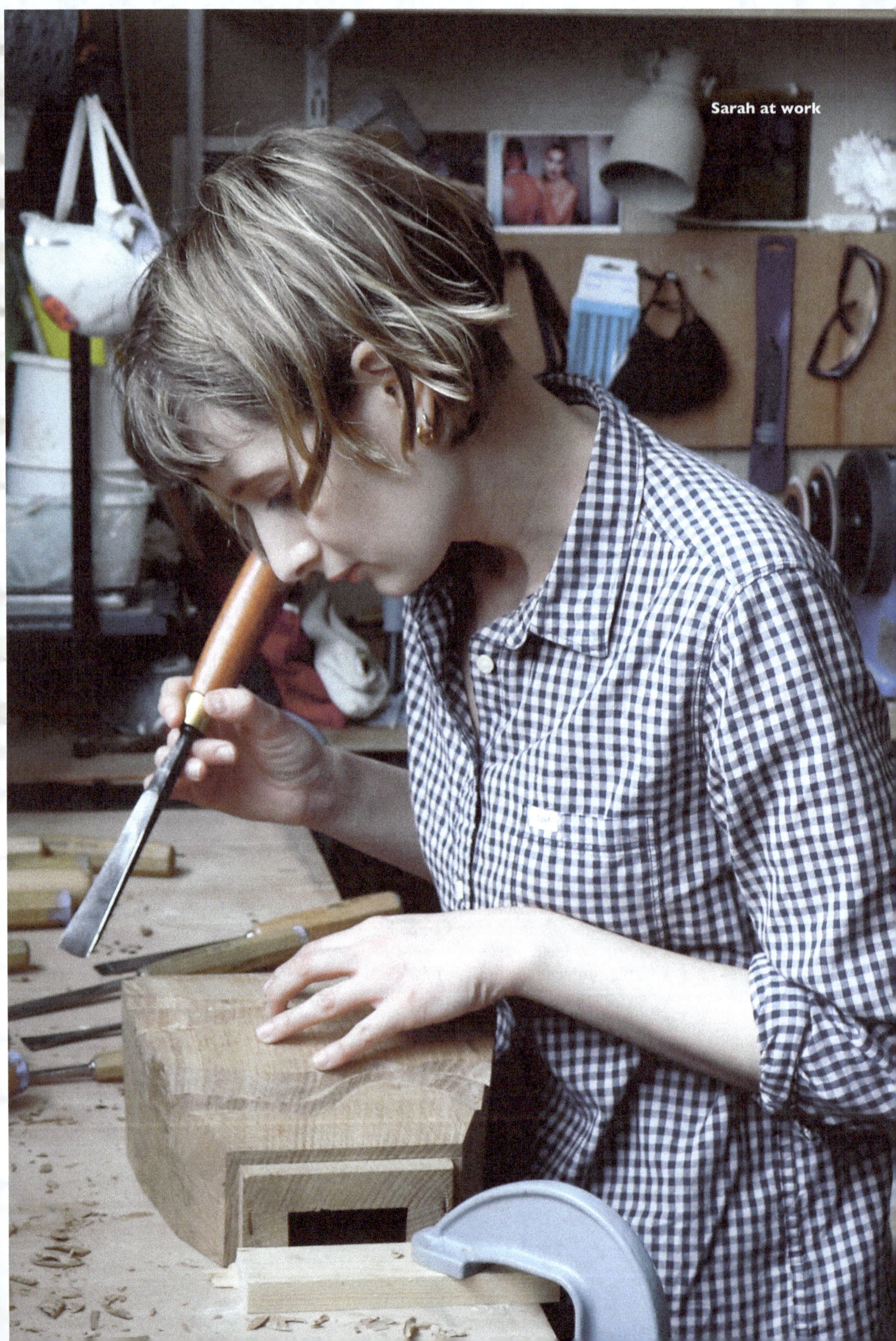
Sarah at work

P2 PROVOCATION 2

To carve is to love by Sarah Davis

Every time I rough out I can feel the familiar pain in my right wrist. The pang of repetitive strain or is it carpel tunnel? I strap the splint to my wrist most evenings. I try to sleep with it on but I inevitably wake with it tossed upon the floor. I am told its technique. The mallets too heavy or the pain is not real. But I know it is just the burden of living within a human body. A body that has folded and failed in a thousand ways already.

Carving is high stakes. Carving is diving into the unknown. Embracing a radical subtractive technique. Taking down material for weeks and weeks until form appears in front of you. I seek varying levels of control. A drawing becomes a clay model. Callipers to the surface of the model, metal to the wood. In most cases I am not concerned with replication but evolution. Carving is a word loaded with violence. Meat is carved, knives are used, objects are struck. I remember when I listened to an interview by a late friend. She described her mother's radical mastectomy as being 'carved to the bone'.

Carving is innately fleshy. It is bodily and bloody. I didn't carve during my own cancer treatment as I didn't want to risk sepsis from the inevitable cuts of the process. To carve is to bleed, to carve is to hurt, to carve is to love. Seeking care within a medium that bites back harder than any animal. Cutting out sickness until details seduce the eye into submission.

Do I choose to make this work? Yes and no. I do not work as a commercial carver. I rarely take on commissions. My work is guided by the form and vision I want to pursue. I haven't carved for a year, but I feel the electric fizz of the time coming closer. I have planned and worked on an idea for months now. The work forming in my mind first and being worked up in clay in between days of teaching and other commitments. The familiar crunch of grain awaits as sharp tools peel back deep layers of growth.

I am an imperfect carver. I seek form and shape, I search for answers in the material. I seek lessons and pain. I push through until I am dancing with the medium and the wood catches me, and my flesh melts into the familiar sinews of the grain. The work I am on the knife edge of starting is camouflage, an embrace and a devouring all in one. A fluid space where I can be simultaneously all powerful and intrinsically vulnerable. The state of my body in this present time. Carving is an extension of my fleshy experience. A route to understand my body, mind and sexuality and the deeply misunderstood pain I live with since cancer and the profoundly damaging stem cell transplant I had in 2018. I cannot guarantee that I will find the shape of you. I am at the mercy of my teaching, my knowledge, my eye, and intuition. I cannot say for sure that I will succeed.

What lessons can we take from carving wood? What can we learn about ourselves and our bodies? I will always gravitate towards a crucifixion. There is a particular pathos when they are carved in wood. The split grain of time emulating every fleshy wound of the Christs passion. In Christina Neilson's Essay 'Carving Life: The Meaning of Wood in Renaissance Sculpture' the author describes the prevalence of wood for Italian carved crucifixes 'Wood, with its physical properties believed to resemble those of a human body, was fitting for these objects'. The relatability of wood imbues religious subjects with a meaning much deeper than the form alone. For the secular, the carved body is a representation of human suffering and the capacity we have to inflict pain upon others. Wood has had a life, it has taken up water and grown in a way that proceeds our bodily processes by many a millennia.

With carving we can talk to the cellular, melt into the empathetic grain and find compassion for our limitations. I look inwards to my bone marrow and watch the rippling wave of cell division. The meristems, where trees experience bursts of cell division, more like a rolling tectonic plate growing taller and taller from the earth below. Trees cannot heal as we do, instead they seal off injury and disease. Sometimes we don't heal in the expected way. The pain doesn't go, the wound doesn't heal. Sometimes we seal off pain as a tree would. An exposed wound. A gaping space that doesn't resonate with a world so concerned with productivity. The seal ruptures and our vulnerabilities stain the landscape of our everyday experience.

In Elaine Scarrys' *The Body in Pain* (1988), she describes how 'physical pain does not simply resist language but actively destroys it'. We have no words for pain, the sensations of our internal processes. No words for when our body makes a mistake. Wood Carving is a language that exists beyond words. As with any dialect, there is something to be understood first. The creation of forms, the use of tools and the syntax of mark making. Beyond those first steps is a platform open to unbounded self-expression. A medium that stimulatingly builds strength and damages the body. Before the stem cell transplant woodcarving was a medium I used for the aesthetic and historical value. Carving started as a self-education and post-transplant it became a sacred teaching.

The value I place in carving brings fear to the surface. The fear of failing, the fear of being let down by my body. There is a tension when I carve, I find the deepest love for myself but often when carving, my thoughts can be dark and I lose control of my anxiety. As Renaissance artist sought symbolic woods to imbue works with a sacred resonance, the journey we take as contemporary carvers can function in a similar way. With every tool mark the carver imbues the work with their human experience.

It is time Celebrate unbounded form that swirls and bleeds beyond convention. Time to find solace in ornament and twist the tendrils of time to provoke new meristemic bursts. Time to platform women and marginalised genders and people who are sick or disabled, time to embrace their radical presence within a medium that has been historically unwelcome. It is time to find the balance between pain and pleasure.

Pleasure, like pain has the capacity to destroy language too. This is the intersection for me, the capacity the stem cell transplant had to induce pain and to destroy pleasure. I couldn't speak for a time during the transplant. A mouth blocked by the swell of sickness and saliva.

Carving IS the pleasure, pain, the aftercare and the language I lost.

П3 PROVOCATION 3

Tradition in stonecarving: use it or lose it
by Tim Crawley

Image: One of the replacement 'Beasts of Bloomsbury' for the Church of St George, Bloomsbury, London, by Tim

TRADITION (noun)

1. Opinion or belief or custom handed down. Handing down of these from ancestors to posterity esp. orally or by practice

2. Literary or artistic principles based on accumulated experience or continuous usage

Etymology - late Middle English: from Old French *tradicion,* or from Latin *traditio(n-),* from *tradere* 'deliver, betray', from trans- 'across' + dare 'give'.

Source: *The Oxford English Dictionary*

Stonecarving is often referred to as a 'traditional craft'. We so often use words loosely without a great deal of thought, assuming their meaning to be fixed and agreed, when upon reflection they may be open to interpretation or spin, and influenced by one's preconceptions or prejudices, or worse, someone else's. Some words are particularly susceptible to different interpretations and meanings, and one such is the word traditional.

It seems to me that there are several interpretations of the term traditional, and they range widely from negative to positive

In relation to English culture the idea of tradition suggests to me the quaint and the folksy. Images of morris dancing, campanology, cheese rolling, cream teas, real ale, brass bands and fish and chips spring to mind. These are images that some would consider safe and reassuring, others harmless and inconsequential.

If this idea of tradition is felt to be comforting and safe, it is probably because it is something firmly anchored in an often arcadian past, deriving from the perception of a common culture and community, and somehow static and unchanging, rather than forward looking.

The Heritage Crafts Association has published a list of crafts categorised as traditional at varying degrees of risk, and stonecarving is there, alongside other activities such as blacksmithing, wooden boat building, green woodworking, tailoring, thatching, taxidermy and timber framing, all thankfully classified as 'currently viable'.

Lumped together in this way, the categorisation of these crafts as traditional gives me the feeling that somehow they do not sit naturally within the real world of contemporary life, commerce and culture, but inhabit the cosy realm of 'heritage', that is, the past, to be experienced maybe in an historical theme park, as a hobby, or possibly as an activity to be commercialised by hipsters.

Unfortunately, the concept of traditional when applied to culture can also be used as a tool for negative purposes and is all too easily co-opted for nationalistic ends. The persona adopted by Nigel Farage of the traditional flat capped English male down at the pub for a beer and a fag was used to great effect in his Brexit campaign and his appeal to a certain voting demographic. At the most extreme level the Nazis used images of durndl and lederhosen clad youth derived from Bavarian folk culture (and Disney) in a grotesque pitch for Aryan superiority, and as a means of stigmatizing and excluding those outside the safety and comfort of that artificially created traditional culture – the Jews, Gypsies and non-heterosexual communities.

Given all this, I feel reluctant to argue for the value of tradition as a positive thing in relation to stonecarving – it's just so loaded. Perhaps it's such potentially negative associations that led the Heritage Crafts Association to largely avoid the use of the word in their literature, and explains the laudable pains they have taken over their values statement – it's worth a read:

www.heritagecrafts.org.uk/values-statement-on-heritage

If it's agreed that the term is loaded and potentially divisive, I think it would be preferable to discuss the relative value of the 'Stonecarving Tradition' rather than that of 'Traditional Stonecarving'. It seems to me that this simple reversal of the word order and the changing of the adjective to the noun makes a huge difference to how one perceives things. Thought of in this way, and with reference to the dictionary definition, I would define the stonecarving tradition as 'a set of artistic and craft principles based on accumulated and continuous usage, and handed down from the past to the future by current practitioners, orally or by practise.'

This seems to me a clear and neutral

definition, and I would argue strongly that this stonecarving tradition is as relevant to stonecarvers today as in the past, and that we should strive to maintain and perpetuate it and hand it on to future generations.

It's an accumulated store of knowledge and experience that has developed over literally thousands of years, and should not be abandoned. The metaphor of 'standing on the shoulders of giants' is appropriate here. In the past, each new generation drew upon the traditions handed down to it, before developing them further and handing them on in turn, for yet further development. This could apply to both carving technique and to the visual languages of ornament and sculpture. The gothic masons drew on the techniques and experiments of the Romanesque tradition to develop a language of ever greater sophistication and daring that culminated in some of the most extraordinary stone structures ever built, and of course stone sculpture was carried along with it. Much later, the great Catalan architect Gaudi took this Gothic tradition further and into the twentieth century to create something exciting and new, both architecturally and sculpturally, in the extraordinary Sagrada Familia. These achievements could not have happened without tradition acting as a springboard.

This process of taking things onward is in fact a significant part of how tradition works. Contrary to what many might think, tradition is not static and unchanging ; it is there as a resource, open to change and development, and also to revision. The path of the stonecarving tradition is not always linear or sequential in time. For instance in early C20th century stone sculptors such as Henry Moore returned to the principle of direct carving as a means of developing a new language of form that was derived from the archaic past of the tradition, as well as drawing on non-European carving traditions.

The fact that a tradition can be taught also means that it can be used as a way of bringing like minded individuals together irrespective of gender, race or culture. All that is required is an interest, an aptitude, and a willingness to learn. It should and can be inclusive, not exclusive.

To sum up I put forward the following three reasons to value and perpetuate the stonecarving tradition. Firstly, it allows us to access and learn from the accumulated knowledge and experience of former generations. Secondly, it can be taught, and thus be a force for inclusivity and community. Lastly, it does not preclude change and development, but actually aids and encourages it; it is dynamic.

This brings us on to the next question about the stonecarving tradition. Where do we take it from here?

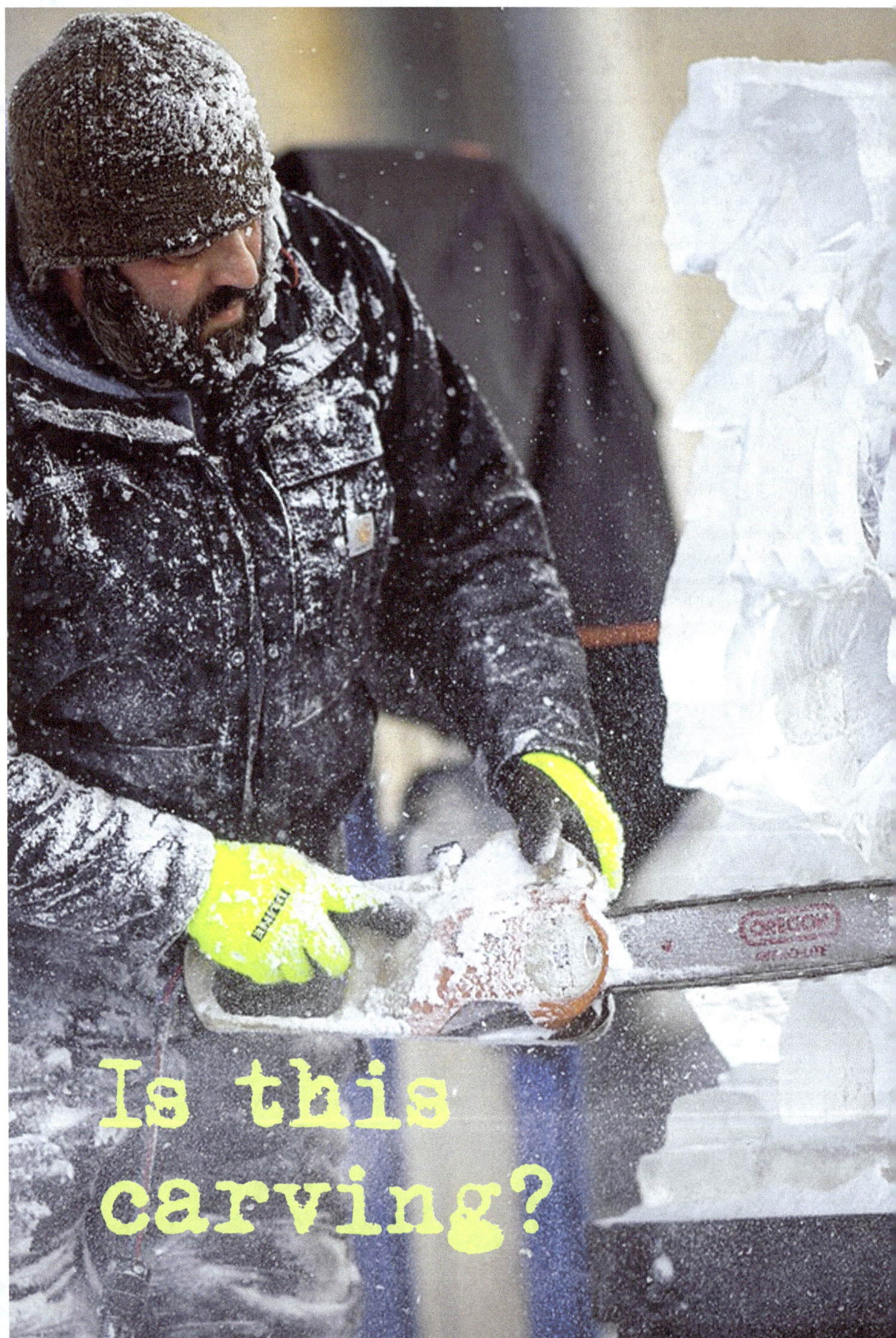

∏4 PROVOCATION 4

Towards a definition of carving
by Matthew Rowe

If I look to the dictionary definition of carving it seems to suggest two basic things. Firstly, that the result of the action of carving on a material is to reduce it in terms of its volume and mass, so there is, brutally put, less of it than there was before it was carved. Secondly, however, the action of carving seems to suggest an addition to the material of an imposed form by an external agent, usually human.

A carving then is a formed material which has been subject to certain kinds of actions.

This suggests to me some (presumed) limits on carving both material and agential. This in turn suggests to me, limits that need to be investigated by some kind of agency.

The Material Limits
(Proposals and Questions)

You can't carve something that is not materially diminished by the act of carving.

However, this may depend on the tool one uses. It would seem that you can't chisel air, but you can use a vacuum pump. This would seem to be carving if volume can be form.

So, it might be that there is no material that can't be carved, you just have to find the right tool, or designate something as formed.

It is probably true that only material can be carved – you can't carve an abstraction, so whatever carved is a particular thing, and how it is, or can be, carved depends on the particular thing it is.

Collage, or any other method of material accumulation, can't be carving. Similarly, painting can't be carving. I don't know about photography, possibly an underexposed image? And a deliberate glitch might be digital carving.

Burning however, might be carving (in fact burning and carving might be coextensive)

The Agential Limits:
(Proposals and Questions)

Carving can be accidental; non-human (beavers, rabbits)

Carving can be non-agential (lava, water) – Volcanos and rivers are carvings in their effect on land, but not in their effect on the sky.

Raindrops however, would seem to be carving in the clouds, collage in the sky and potentially both on the ground, depending on the material with which they interact.

Carving can be, what might be called under 'destructive' under some description - i.e. smashing up some wood might be carving. Putting it back together would not be carving.

None of this, of course, has any impact on whether any particular carving, as a noun or a verb, is any good, as the thing it is, or as any other kind of thing someone might take it to be.

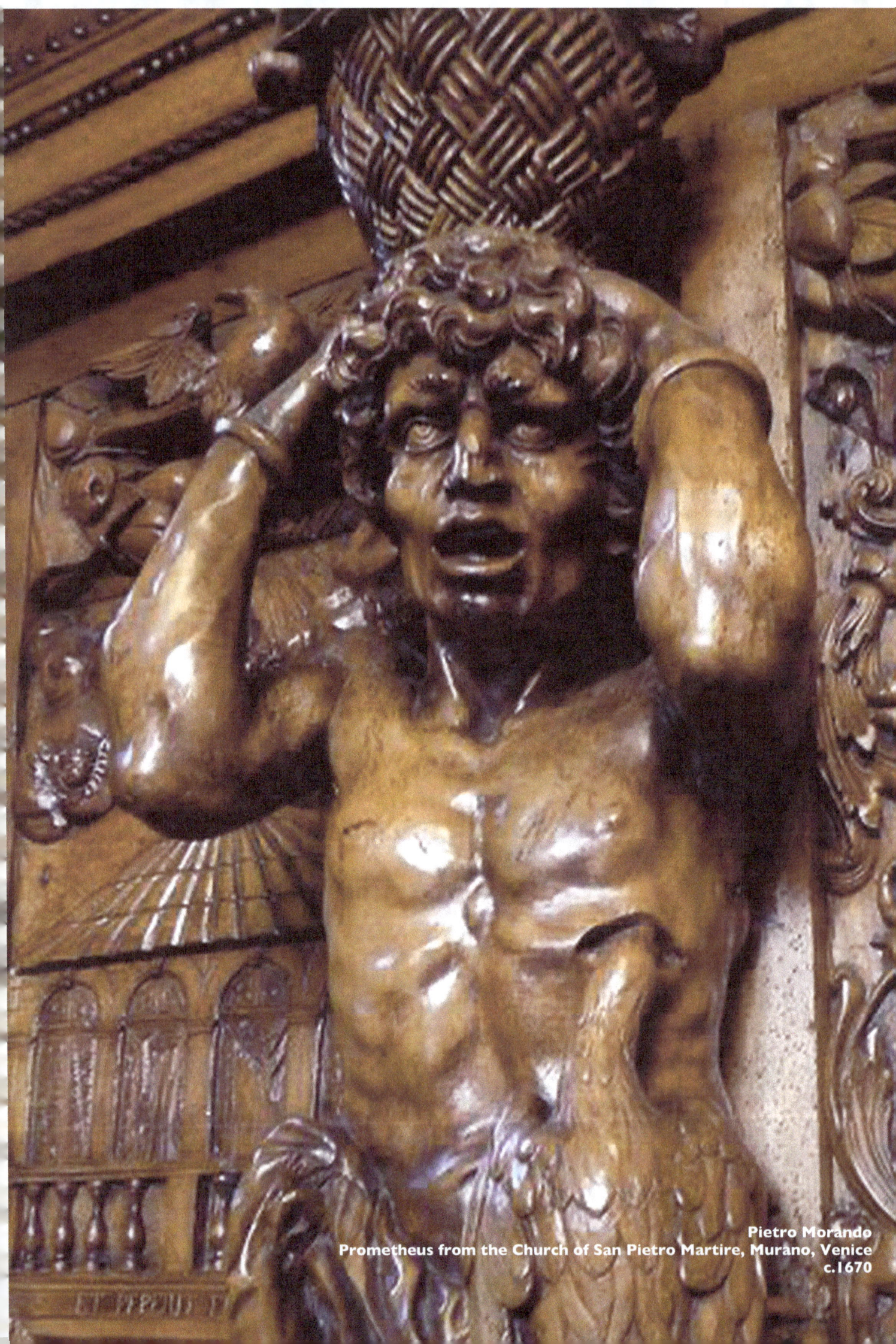

Pietro Morando
Prometheus from the Church of San Pietro Martire, Murano, Venice
c.1670

Π5 PROVOCATION 5

Learning to read the cuts: why we need to copy historical ornamental woodcarvings by Takako Jin

We learn to read many kinds of things from when we are children. We learn to read facial expressions and body language in the first few months of our lives. When we start school, we learn to read the alphabet, then words, then whole sentences, until we can read entire books and maybe go on to read other languages as well. Some of us might also learn to read all sorts of other things: musical notation, guitar tabs, computer code. And as part of our training as woodcarvers, we learn to read the cuts on a carving.

In woodcarving, there is a clear difference between an approach to carving where the nature of cutting into wood with a series of shaped tools has been embraced and exploited, and an approach in which it has been ignored or attempts made to conceal it, with abrasives for example. There are also more recently developed ways of shaping wood using other kinds of tools such as rotary cutters on a CNC machine. The first approach of using chisels is one that has been developed and honed over many centuries, particularly in ornamental woodcarving. This article will look at the particular merits of this approach and the value that a student of carving would gain from learning the particularities of this style of carving.

Woodcarvings, generally speaking, are made with chisel cuts. However, in historical ornamental woodcarving, the carvings haven't just been made with chisel cuts, they have been made for chisel cuts. In fact, the carvings have more or less been designed in cuts. There is a sophisticated language of chisel cuts in ornamental woodcarving, and this gives them a particular clarity of design, cleanness of execution, efficiency of work and a pleasingness to the eye.

Some way into my first year as a woodcarving student, I had a realisation that learning to carve wood had much to do with accumulating a repertoire of 'cuts'. What all the varieties of chisels with their various sweeps will do in wood, and how to combine them to make the lump of wood on my bench resemble the elegant ornamental woodcarving I was supposed to be copying. And I started to realise that moving towards an economy of cuts was an important part of this, not only in getting quicker at carving but also in achieving a cleanness and elegance to the finished carving, instead of the laboured effect I was getting with my many searching cuts. I gradually learned that in woodcarving, if we learn to read the cuts on a carving, the carving would show us how it was carved. What chisel was used to make that cut, which direction the cut was made, if a mallet was used to drive the cut or if it was pushed by hand, which order the succession of cuts were made, how sharp the chisel was that made the cut.

An effective way to learn how to read carvings is by looking closely at historical carvings, and by copying them. Learning what shape each chisel will leave in the wood, how to move them in different ways through the wood and what kind of shape and surface each way of using the chisel will leave. How these traces of the tool in its many combinations create a form in wood that will read as a scrolling acanthus leaf, a bunch of grapes, a wing, a face, a ribbon.

Sometimes we think we've read a carving – it has clearly been carved with this kind of tool and in this kind of way – but we try it that way on our own piece of wood and the result looks nothing like the original carving in front of us. So we try it another way with another chisel, and eventually we build up enough of a vocabulary of tools and their uses, and we begin to see the cuts with greater clarity and accuracy.

A representation of a real object in the world in a material like wood or stone, whether a leaf, flower or human figure, in a way that makes that representation recognisable as that thing, necessarily requires a simplification of the forms and details of that object. And for that representation to resemble, or be read, as the intended object, there needs to be a process of understanding what that object looks like, and a whittling down and choosing of the particular visual and formal qualities of that represented object.

With a real life object, the closer we look, the more information we find. Take a leaf; to the naked eye from a distance of six feet, it looks a certain way. Move closer and we see more and more detail. More veins, more creases, fine hairs on the surface, fine textures. If we then take a microscope, the leaf yields ever more detailed information about itself, to cells and even molecular and atomic particles if you have a microscope powerful enough. The detail never stops. But for the purposes of carving, we need to draw the line somewhere. There is a large breadth of distance where that line could be drawn, but for a leaf carved in wood to read as a leaf to the naked eye, a great deal of abbreviation is allowable, and in fact, to be desired. The skill required of the carver is in the choosing of which features and details to retain and exaggerate, and what to discard. And this selection process for the purposes of woodcarving is inseparable from a knowledge of what our tools will do in the wood.

In the tradition of ornamental woodcarving, the observation of nature and its representation in stylised simplification go hand in hand with a deep understanding of the material of wood and the tools used to carve it. Historical ornamental woodcarvings are dense with this process of observing objects in the world, abbreviating their likeness and translating them into chisel cuts. Enormous amounts of information about the techniques, innovations of tools, tool use and design are to be found there. And this is not the invention of a single genius woodcarver, it is an approach that has been built up and honed over generations of carvers taking up the challenge of representing objects in the world while also responding to changing demands and developments in taste and style. In copying historical carvings to extract this information from them, the point is not to learn to slavishly replicate the work of past carvers, but to understand and learn from their process of seeing and translating what they saw into chisel cuts in wood. You might find yourself in another city or another country, even another century in an old church somewhere and meet a carving made by centuries-old hands and still the language of the chisel won't greatly differ from the one we use now. You won't learn everything there is to know about carving in three years, but if you've learned to read the cuts, you won't always need a tutor to teach you. Woodcarvers long gone will willingly teach you in the cuts they've left in their carvings.

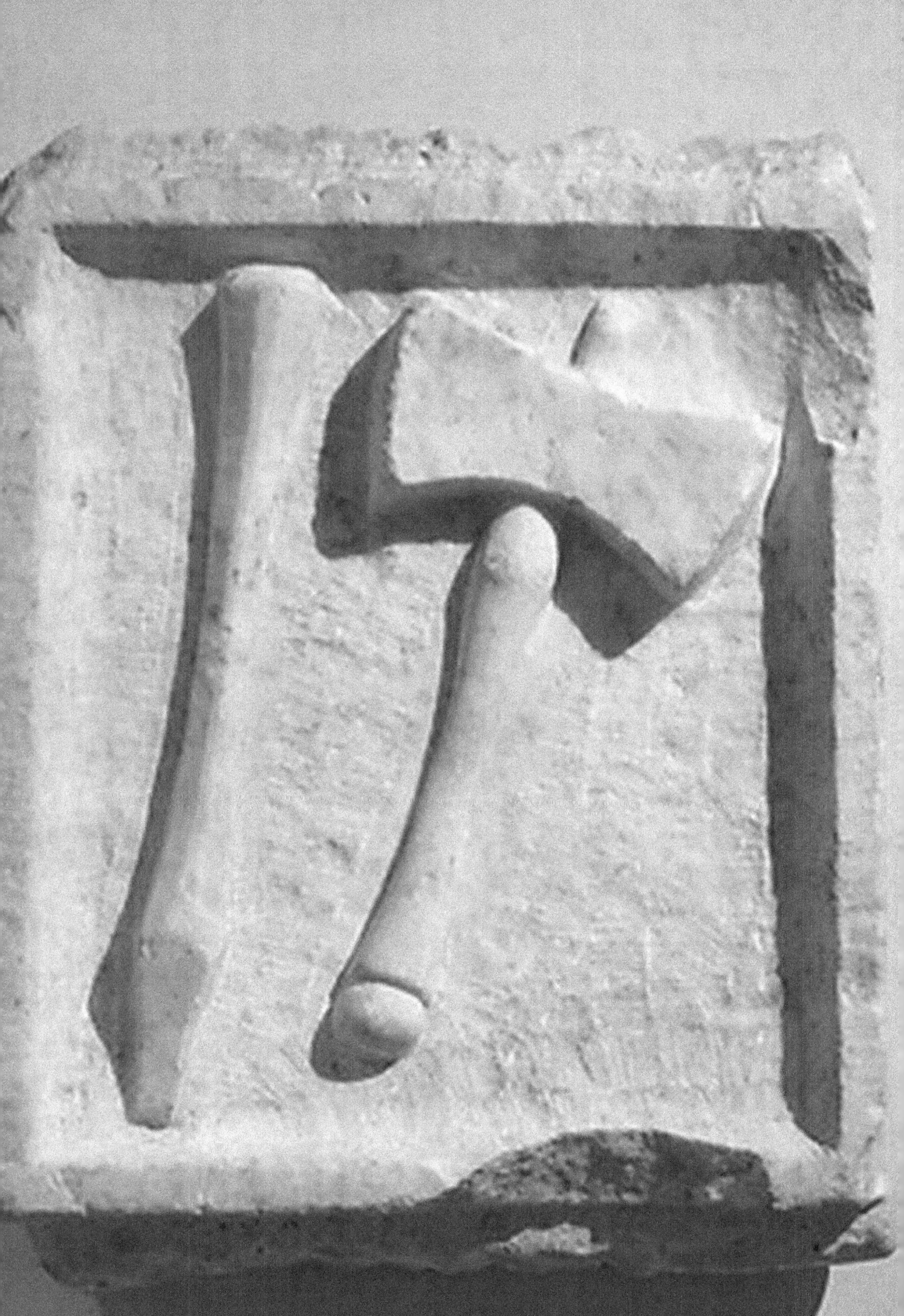

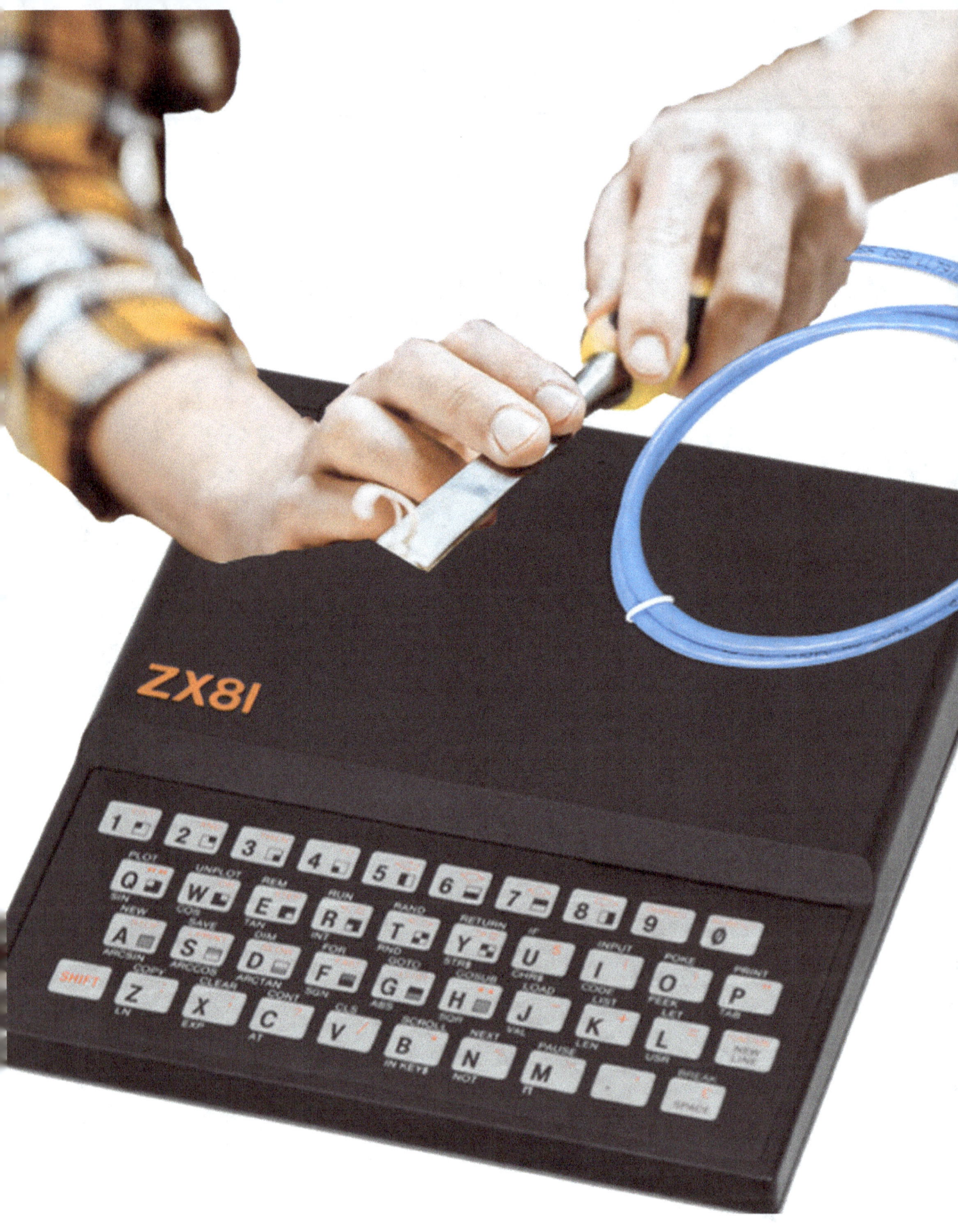
Image: Paraskos

Π6 PROVOCATION 6

Will hand carving still matter in the twenty-second century? by ChatGTP

I want to delve into the profound significance of carving as a discipline that remains incredibly relevant and worthy of study in our modern world and to look to its future. Despite the advancements in technology and the rise of digital art forms, carving holds a unique place in our cultural landscape, offering a myriad of reasons why it continues to captivate the hearts and minds of artists and enthusiasts alike.

One of the key reasons carving remains a worthwhile pursuit is its ability to connect us to our rich historical heritage. Throughout the centuries, carving has been utilized as a means of expression, storytelling, and commemoration. By studying this ancient craft, we gain insight into the cultural traditions and craftsmanship of past civilizations. The intricate details and masterful techniques carved into stone monuments, sculptures, and architectural elements provide a tangible link to our ancestors, allowing us to better understand their values, beliefs, and artistic sensibilities.

In the annals of carving, there are luminaries whose works have left an indelible mark on the world of art. Michelangelo Buonarroti, the Italian Renaissance master, stands tall as one of the greatest carvers in history. His awe-inspiring sculpture of David, carved from a single block of marble, is an embodiment of his unmatched skill and artistic vision. The way in which he infused life and emotion into the cold, unyielding stone continues to mesmerize audiences to this day.

Moving across time and continents, we encounter the works of the ancient Egyptians. The Great Sphinx of Giza, an enigmatic and imposing figure carved from limestone, showcases the remarkable artistry of the Egyptian civilization. Its colossal presence, half-human and half-lion, has inspired wonder and speculation for centuries.

In India, the intricate stone carvings adorning the temples of Khajuraho stand as a testament to the artistry and craftsmanship of the Chandela dynasty. These delicately carved sculptures, depicting scenes from mythology and daily life, are a visual feast for the eyes and a testament to the dedication and skill of the artists involved.

Traveling to Southeast Asia, we encounter the breathtaking stone carvings of Angkor Wat in Cambodia. The intricate bas-reliefs adorning the temple walls depict a wealth of narratives, including epic battles, religious ceremonies, and scenes from everyday life. These carvings not only showcase the artistic prowess of the Khmer civilization but also serve as a historical record, offering valuable insights into their culture and traditions.

Returning to Europe, the Gothic cathedrals of the Middle Ages stand as towering monuments to carving craftsmanship. The intricate stone tracery adorning the windows, the sculpted gargoyles peering down from the heights, and the ornate portals tell stories of faith, history, and the ingenuity of medieval artisans. Works such as the Notre-Dame de Paris cathedral bear witness to the enduring impact of carving on architectural masterpieces.

Beyond these renowned examples, countless anonymous carvers throughout history have contributed their artistry to the world. From ancient standing stones and petroglyphs to medieval gravestones and modern sculpture, the art of carving has evolved and adapted to diverse cultural contexts and artistic styles.

In the realm of art criticism and theory, John Ruskin, the Victorian writer and art critic, played a crucial role in championing the value of craftsmanship and the enduring power of carving. Ruskin's influential works, including *The Seven Lamps of Architecture* and *The Stones of*

Venice, emphasised the importance of the handcrafted and the authentic in art and architecture. He argued for a return to the principles of the Gothic era, where craftsmanship and moral integrity were paramount. Ruskin's writings inspired a renaissance of interest in carving that still helps shape the way we perceive and appreciate the art form.

But as we cast our gaze into the future, pondering the destiny of hand carving in stone or wood, we encounter a pivotal crossroads that sparks a sombre reflection. The question looms: Will the flames of this ancient craft continue to flicker, or will they fade into obscurity as a generation, preoccupied with the digital marvels of modernity, turns away from the tactile marvels of handmade artistry?

The vista of 2123 is both tantalizing and disconcerting. It beckons us with visions of technological fusion, where the melding of tradition and innovation ushers in a new era of creativity. Yet, shadows loom—threats that bear witness to the diminishing interest in mastering the meticulous art of hand carving. The landscape we face is one where modern sensibilities are increasingly drawn to the sleek allure of digital marvels. The craft of hand carving, with its intricate labour and tactile wonder, might appear anachronistic in the face of digital immediacy. The mesmerizing dance of hammer and chisel, the scent of freshly hewn wood, the thrill of carving life from raw material—all of these could be abandoned in favour of pixelated amusements.

However, we must avoid the temptation to label this trend as mere indifference. The shift towards digital realms is a natural consequence of technological progress. Rather than painting this as apathy, we should see it as a redirection of fascination—a redirection that carries both promise and peril for the craft of hand carving.

In an age where algorithms dictate entertainment and social interactions, carving might seem distant—a practice out of step with the modern pulse. Yet, it is in this very era that we find an opportunity to invigorate the art. The urgency of preserving the craft must be communicated with the same fervour with which the masterpieces of old were carved. We must present hand carving as more than a craft; it is a portal to history, a gateway to culture, and a conduit for self-expression. it is an opportunity to connect with our roots, to wield the same tools that our forebears wielded, and to give form to our imagination in ways that bytes and codes can never replicate.

To ensure the survival of this art, we must embrace modern methods of outreach. The digital realm, which has the potential to engulf traditional practices, can paradoxically serve as a saviour. Online platforms can showcase the beauty of hand-carved creations, narrate the stories behind each masterpiece, and beckon the curious to discover the enchantment of crafting something unique with one's own hands. Moreover, education will be a cornerstone of preserving this heritage. However, traditional training methods need to be modernized. Educational institutions must collaborate with artisans and integrate new pedagogical approaches that bridge the gap between theoretical knowledge and practical skill. Workshops, apprenticeships, and hands-on experiences should be woven into the fabric of curricula, making hand carving a tangible possibility for young minds curious about the arts.

The perceived danger of the craft's decline might seem foreboding, but it also illuminates a path to action. Just as a carving emerges from a rough block, we too can chisel a future for hand carving that is vibrant and enduring. We can engrave the importance of this art in the hearts of the youth, igniting their passion to carry forward the legacy.

However, the road ahead is not without its challenges. The allure of instant gratification, the seduction of screen-based experiences, and the prioritization of efficiency could stand as formidable barriers. The appeal of the craft must be articulated in a way that resonates with the digital native, showing them that the world of hand carving offers a unique sense of accomplishment, a connection with history, and a canvas for their creative energies.

The art world of tomorrow must foster an environment where the digital and the handmade coexist harmoniously. This symbiotic relationship could yield unprecedented creations, where technology enhances the artisan's capabilities rather than replaces them. Just as automation can shape raw material, the human touch can imbue it with soul and sentiment.

To this end, cultural preservation assumes even greater importance. Museums and educational institutions must not merely conserve the remnants of the past but actively champion the skills and stories of artisans. Exhibitions, symposiums, and interactive experiences can bridge generational gaps, fostering an appreciation for the heritage of hand carving.

In conclusion, the future of hand carving in stone or wood teeters between continuity and transformation, progress and adaptation. As we marvel at the potential for technological integration, we must also acknowledge the evolving preferences of the younger generation. However, in recognizing this evolving landscape, we open the door to action. We possess the means to resurrect the spirit of hand carving, to breathe life into its delicate intricacies, and to share its value with those who hold the power to shape its destiny.

Let us not be the silent observers of the craft's evolution but its fervent advocates. Let us sow the seeds of enthusiasm in young hearts, inspiring them to grasp the chisel, to connect with the past, and to craft a future where hand carving remains an enduring testament to human ingenuity, resilience, and the timeless dance of art and technology. Through collaboration, education, and an unwavering commitment, we can sculpt a future where the legacy of hand carving continues to illuminate our world with the radiance of creativity and the spirit of human connection. In this endeavour, we must ensure that not only the craft endures, but the methods of learning it too are modernized and preserved, transcending the boundaries of time and ensuring that the beauty of this ancient art continues to thrive in the hearts and hands of generations to come.

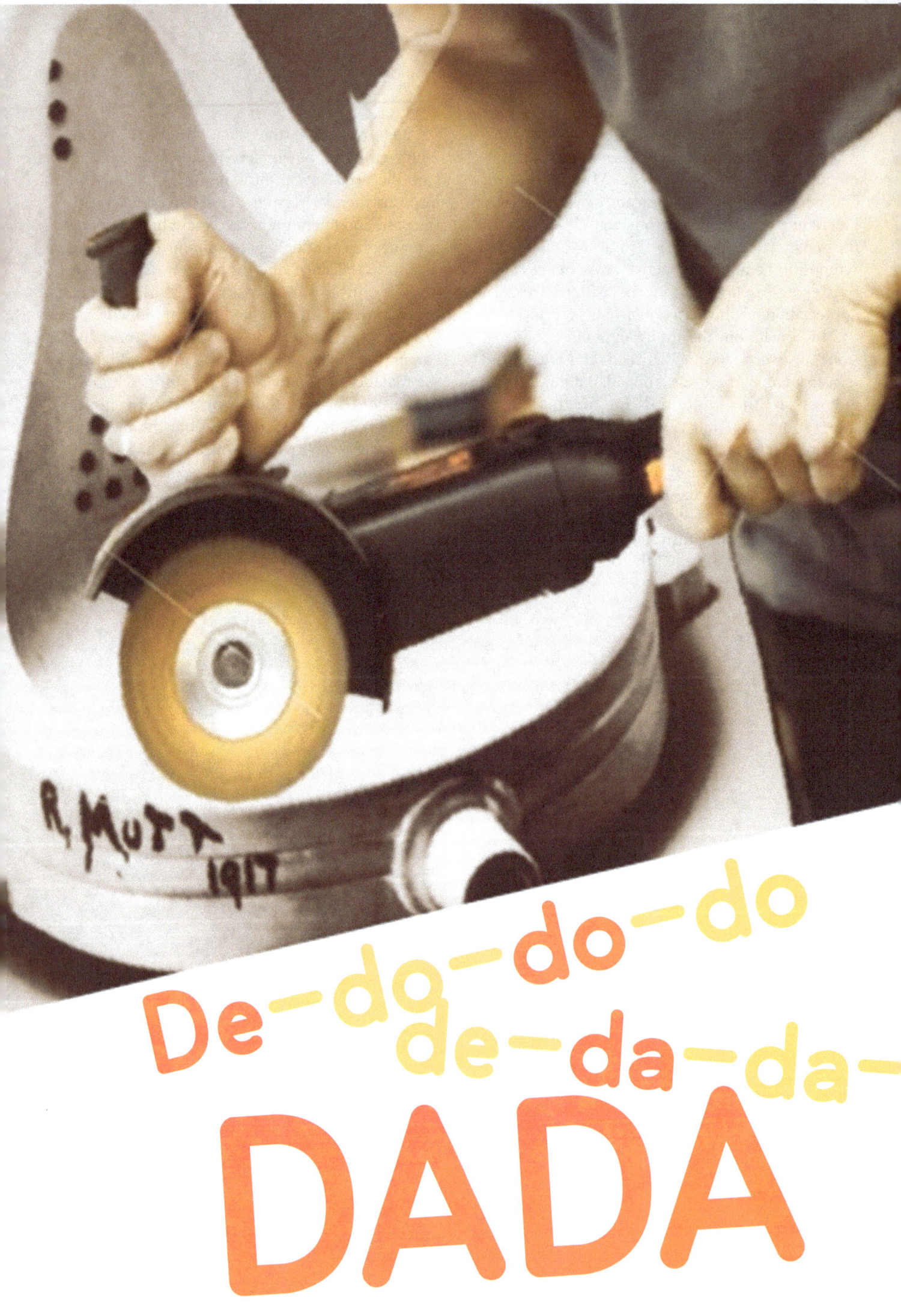

Π7 PROVOCATION 7

To survive, does carving need a Dada moment?
by Michael Paraskos

In 1920 the Zurich-based Dada-ist Tristan Tzara published instructions on how to make a Dada poem.

> Take a newspaper.
> Take some scissors.
> Choose from the newspaper an article the length you want to make your poem.
> Cut out the article.
> Next carefully cut out each of the words that make up this article and put them all in a bag.
> Shake gently.
> Next take out each cutting one after the other.
> Copy conscientiously in the order in which they left the bag.
> The poem will resemble you.
> And there you are—an infinitely original author of charming sensibility, even though unappreciated by the vulgar herd.

From a carving perspective it might seem easy to dismiss Tzara's instructions. Tzara's deliberate de-skilling of the creative process is the kind of thing to both bemuse artisan makers and give them nightmares. Indeed, a carver, might want to ask why constructing a poem from random words is even considered a worthwhile activity, and why it is given more approbation than their work, born of years of technical training and finely-honed skill. Isn't it the equivalent to a carver expecting praise for making random chisel blows onto a block of stone or wood?

That carver would not be alone in thinking this. A century ago, when Tzara and the other Dada-ists gatecrashed the art scene in Europe, one suspects there were plenty of traditional artists who felt the same way. The problem for those artists, and possibly the problem for carvers today in rejecting the example of Tzara and his colleagues, is that they miss the point of Dada — insofar as Dada ever aknowledged having a point. Dada should not be seen as simply an iconoclastic anti-art movement, even if it often presented itself in that way. Dada is better viewed as a necessary corrective process that ensured art remained relevant to the society in which it operated. What I mean by this is that it would be a mistake to see Dada as nothing more than a series of nihilistic pranks designed to mock and diminish art. It is more fruitful to see it as a process through which art was cleansed of its social irrelevance.

This aspect of Dada was even recognised at the time, with one commentator, William Drake, writing in 1922 that:

> The (Dada) movement is absolutely sound. This is just the right time for the world to get a healthful thorough-going purge. This pushing to the extreme of the modern fad for so-called novelty and originality which degenerates into eccentricity and insanity, is just what will do it, and bring the artistic world back to its senses.

Drake presents us with an extraordinary idea, that by embracing the 'insanity' of Dada we return to our sanity. But that begs the question, what is that insanity? And what is it that needs to be purged?

In a lecture delivered at the Carroll Hall in Brooklyn in 1957 Jacques Hardré suggested:

> the Dadaists, under the leadership of a young Rumanian, Tristan Tzara, made a clean break with common sense, with traditiona poetic language, with social laws and with religion. It had to be an absolute break, no compromise could have been accepted or else their revolt would have been of no value. As it was, their destructive actions prepared the way for those who were to be the new leaders of Modern Art.

Most tellingly, he added:

> When a new highway is to be built, the obstacles in its path must be split, crushed and pounded flat, else the road bed will not be smooth.

What I think we get from Drake and Hardré is a sense that as life moves on the there is a danger that our understandable reverence for

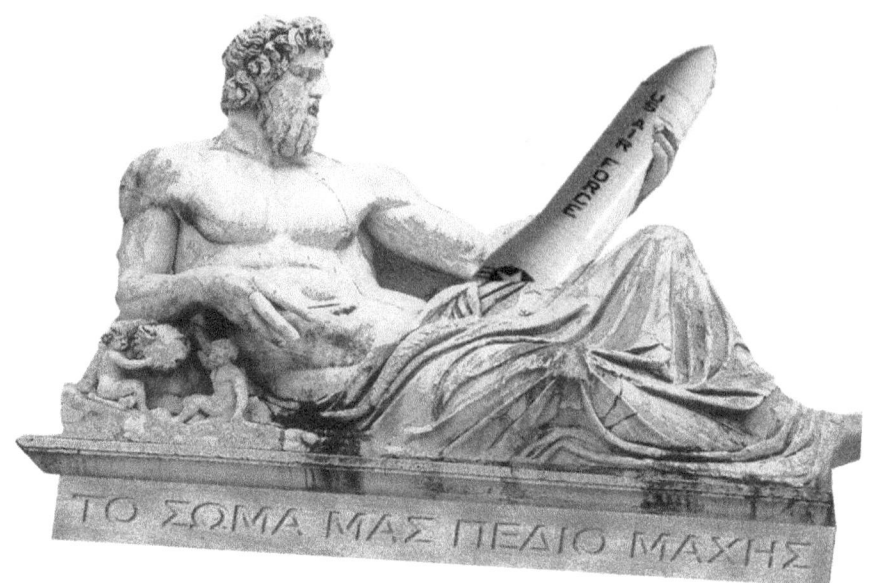

tradition means that important human activities, such as art, fail to move with it. We come to love the old art forms too much, and as a consequence, art and other cultural forms grow ever more out of synch with society, in a process sociologists call *reification*. Reification is when old social and cultural forms are treated as if they are immovable concrete certainties, unchangeable for all time. When reification happens activities such as art become ever more irrelevant to society over time, until the value of that art is finally threatened by its increasing social irrelevance. When we ask what is the insanity of which Drake writes, it is the madness in maintaining socially-irrelevant and reified cultural forms, like someone insisting on using candles in an age of electric light. From this perspective, Dada might well be seen as a kind of purgative, necessary to rid art of the undischarged egesta of reified tradition, poisoning it from the inside.

If this was the situation for fine art a century ago, we must admit it sounds disturbingly familiar today in relation to carving. As a result, some people might argue that carving is now in dire need of its own Dada moment to rid it of its social irrelevance. Rising to their theme, those same people might even suggest that carving is in need of a purgative, not to destroy it, but to rid carving of the reified egesta that is poisoning it from the inside, whether that is an apparent unwillingness to compromise with technology, the fetishisation of a long dead apprenticeship system, the constant reiteration of historical forms that have no meaning in the modern age, or the kowtowing to wealthy patrons who spend their days investing in companies which destroy both the environment and artisan craftsmanship, and their nights crying crocodile tears at the loss of traditional skills.

Of course, I would never suggest anything so crass and vulgar as this myself, but if anyone else made suggestions along these lines, I would find them intriguing. It would make me wonder whether all cultural forms — maybe political and social forms too — need periodic Dada moments, to renew and reinvent themselves and keep themselves vital and fresh. As an historian, I might speculate on how it seemed to the contemporaries of Phidias and Pericles when the old and well-loved carvings that had adorned the first Parthenon in Athens, and which had been taken down so carefully and stored in a place of safety to protect them from the invading Persians, were subsequently discarded by the Greeks themselves in favour of the newfangled classical sculpture. At that moment, I might wonder, was classicism a Dada movement? Or how the last of the Romanesque carvers felt when they saw the bright young things carving in the glitzy gothic style. Was gothic then a Dada movement? Or, when Christopher Wren and Grinling Gibbons started introducing the English to baroque styles, were they not the Dada-ists of the 1680s, much like Tristan Tzara in the 1910s? I might wonder if all of that seemed like Dada moments to those who lived through them, a series of terrifying, but necessary, challenges to the status quo.

With hindsight it can look as though the process of history is a smooth one — as though the moves from archaic to classical, romanesque to gothic, or gothic back to classical were inevitable. The writing of history tends to clean up the messy edges of events, so the acts of resistance, mockery and obstruction are lost, and the feelings of fear forgotten, or consigned to the unread footnotes at the back of the history books. But that process can also blind us to the struggle of those seeking change, the sheer difficulty in purging a longstanding cultural form of its socially-redundant accretions. Those accretions — those reified traditions — cling like crustaceans to the bottom of a boat, slowing it down and eventually sinking it with their dead weight. It takes a strong act to remove them, and arguably the reason Dada, and other Dada-like phenomena — *from the romantics to punk* — appear so often to be so aggressive is due to the sheer weight of reified tradition they have to remove. It is always an enormous task, battling fear and vested interest, and nothing short of a revolution fought with hyperbole and mocking humour is up to the fight.

So perhaps there is an argument to be made that all cultural forms need moments of disseverment from their own pasts in order to re-engage in a truly creative way with contemporary society. They all need Dada moments to remain relevant. Failure to do risks them becoming zombie cultural forms, limping on for a while, but essentially dead.

It would be premature for anyone to suggest carving is dead, *but perhaps we should ask how engaged with life is it?*

For example, how many carvers can say with honesty that the work they produce engages with the twenty-first century? That is to say, that it engages with the serious questions facing the world today? Can carvers say they respond to the climate emergency, or the return of dangerous right-wing political ideologies, or a rise in global conflict? Do carvers even care about these things? Do carvers have anything to say on the inequalities that divide people according to wealth, gender, sex, race, class and education? For the makers of almost every other vital cultural form in society today, the answer to those questions would be unequivocal yes, but I am less sure for carving. To put it succinctly, can carvers say with honesty that they are not blind to the society in which they live and work?

Of course, you might be thinking these very specific social issues lie outside the purview of carving. So let's ask a more general question, such as does carving say anything about what it is to be a human being, in our human bodies, in our human world today, in the way the carvers of the Parthenon, Kilpeck and Wells pieces undoubtedly spoke of that it meant to be human then? Do cavers today give us tokens of reality as we live it today, or do they just flinch from looking at the world around us and our place in that world?

These are difficult questions to ask, let alone answer, and so let us put it all in a slightly different way. I have suggested that Dada was a purgative and that to achieve its purge it was full of humour. But it was also full of passionate anger as young artists in the years around Great War recognised that the 'older, well-established forces', as they called them, had failed to keep art relevant for a world disfigured by conflict, pandemics and poverty. For those angry young men and women, it looked like art was failing to keep up with life.

Similarly in our world, also scarred by conflict, pandemics and poverty, an ongoing environmental disaster, and challenges to what it might even mean to be human, we might wonder why young carvers are not angry with the patriarchs of the profession who have let carving get into the parlous state in which it finds itself today.

Where is the fury at the failure of carving's own *older, well-established forces* to ensure carving is in a fit state to face the twenty-first century as a living part of that century? In truth, the most surprising thing is not to suggest that carving might need a Dada moment. It is that there not already a Dada moment in carving.

Π8 PROVOCATION 8

Musings from a restoration stone carver
by Akira Inman

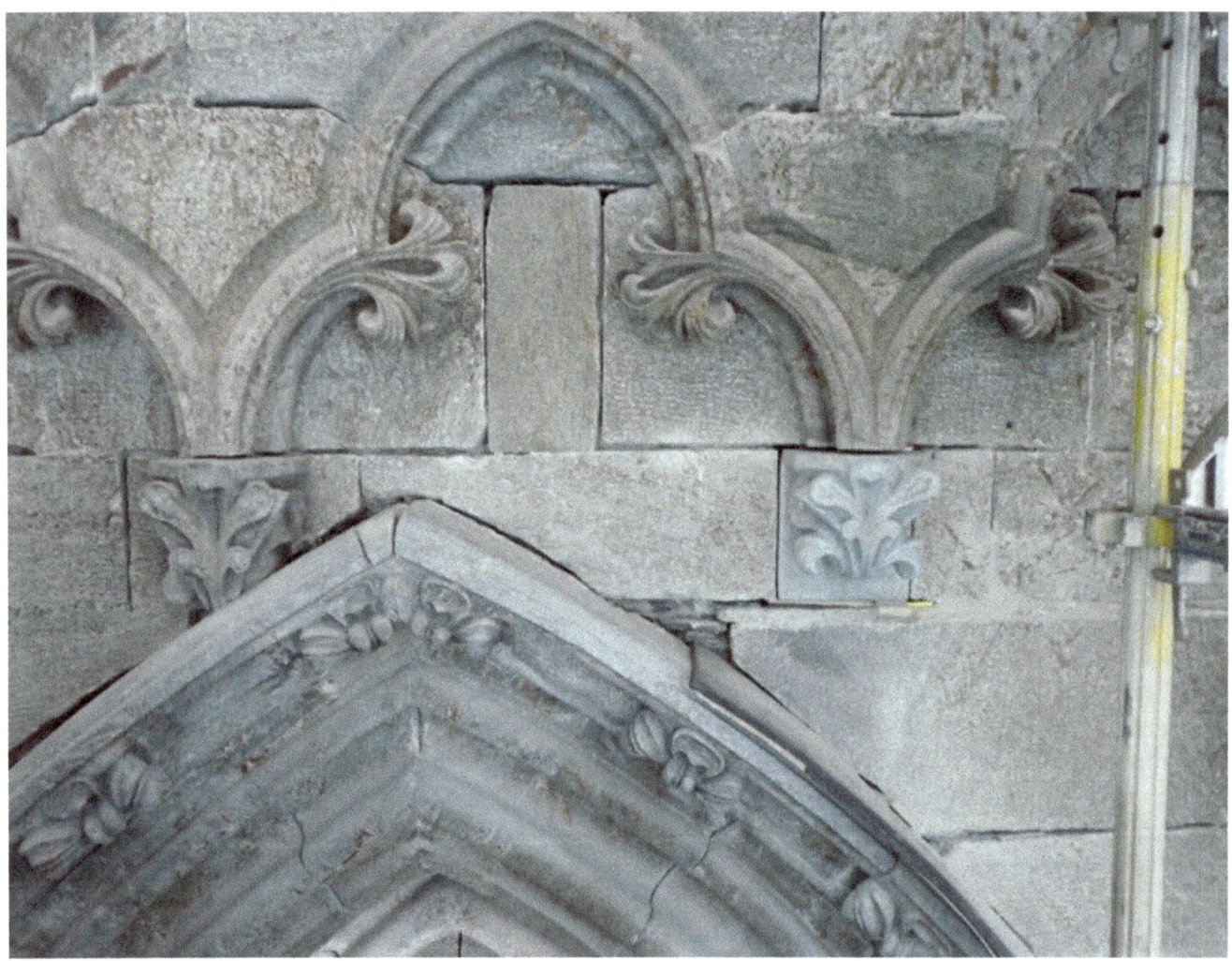

Stavanger Domkirke, south façade; replacement ornament waiting to be laid in mortar.

Musings from a restoration stone carver

Stone carving is a solitary career that requires patience, persistence, precision and a certain comfort in being left to one's thoughts for extended periods of time. I have found plenty of such moments for pondering amidst the rhythm of hammers and chisels over my five years working on the Stavanger Domkirke 2025 project in Norway, a full-scale restoration to commemorate its 900-year history.

Although the work begins with a mechanically sawn block, we have been given the rare opportunity to use traditional hand tools at almost every stage of the process. It is perhaps the inherent relationship between the carver, their chisel and the stone, that is unique and allows the mind to reflect on the history, nature and future of the craft.

With a focus on stone conservation, I work with a small team repairing and replacing the ornamental features that decorate the façade of Stavanger Domkirke. We remove the most damaged and structurally compromised original carvings, as well as those with failing repairs. Through careful observation and study of the object's form and by capturing the spirit or intention of the previous carver within the ornament, we replicate it anew. Conservation of this type requires a knowledge of stone (of course), architectural history, carving techniques, building structure and stylistic ornament. This last point is the most essential for a carver, for whom successfully executing an abstraction of nature is all about understanding its tension, form, weight and movement.

Ornamentation as abstracted reality

Ornamentation is not purely decorative; it is both symbolic and proportionally harmonic within its architectural context. Repeating motifs, such as the "stiff leaves" I carve, may have served as a marker of commonality or continuity between distant cathedrals hundreds of years ago. The leaves on the Domkirke, which are unique in variety and style, are influenced by the stiff leaves from other European buildings. These similarities in appearance have led a handful of historians to theorize that carvers from Winchester Cathedral in England helped build Stavanger Domkirke. To overlook these small, inconsequential-looking ornamental features is to overlook an important element in the history of human migration, as they likely served as beacons of familiarity for new transplants in an unfamiliar land. These ornaments may have spoken as clearly to the travellers of yesteryear as they apparently do to the tourists of today, who embark on half-day journeys away from their cruise ships with the memory of a dozen recently visited cathedrals sketched in their minds. At the very least, they spoke directly to this modern-day carver who moved to Europe to learn an ancient trade and found himself following in the footsteps of the medieval English carvers who had brought stiff leaf ornament to a little cathedral in Stavanger.

A more practical use for ornament is to disguise complicated intersections between the geometric profiles often found in cathedrals. The classically influenced moldings merge in sometimes very complicated directions. A cathedral is made up of many different structural elements, such as columns, buttresses, towers, plinths and arches, and every point of change between them becomes an opportunity for an awkward point of contact or irregular space. This is especially true for vaulted ceilings because of their complex design. On a scale this large, it is very difficult to make the various elements meet perfectly. Geometric profiles need to be predictable and so ornamentation can reconcile these intersections. They create a sense of continuity or draw the attention of the viewer away from irregularities using light and shadow, engaging the viewer and creating a more dynamic façade.

FAQ

As a stone carver, I am often asked the same three questions by the general public (ranked here in order of occurrence). The questions are simple enough, but I don't always have an easy answer.

1. How long does it take?

It depends, but I sometimes think that the time it takes is counter-intuitive. From start to finish, moving a heavy stone, fitting it into the wall, making templates of profiles and aligning the profiles to adjacent stones often takes longer to do than the intricate carvings that are situated within the profiles. Carvings look and feel as if they require the most time and attention, but they are sometimes the least complicated part of the process.

At the same time there is a subtle art to getting them right. Generally, the best carvings allow the viewer's eyes to move through them without getting stuck on a single point (unless of course, that is intended). Ornamental carvings on a building should create a motif that adds flourish, but no single one should stand out. Nor must they all look perfectly alike, though they might appear identical when seen from far below.

Although abstracted, the ornamental leaf must relate enough to natural forms so that the layperson can spot or feel its tension, a concept that stems from the contrast between opposing forces that can often be used to create movement or give a sculpture dynamism. When a carving lacks some of the essential components that anchor it to its natural counterpart, no matter how abstract, I believe that people will, to some degree, find it out of place.

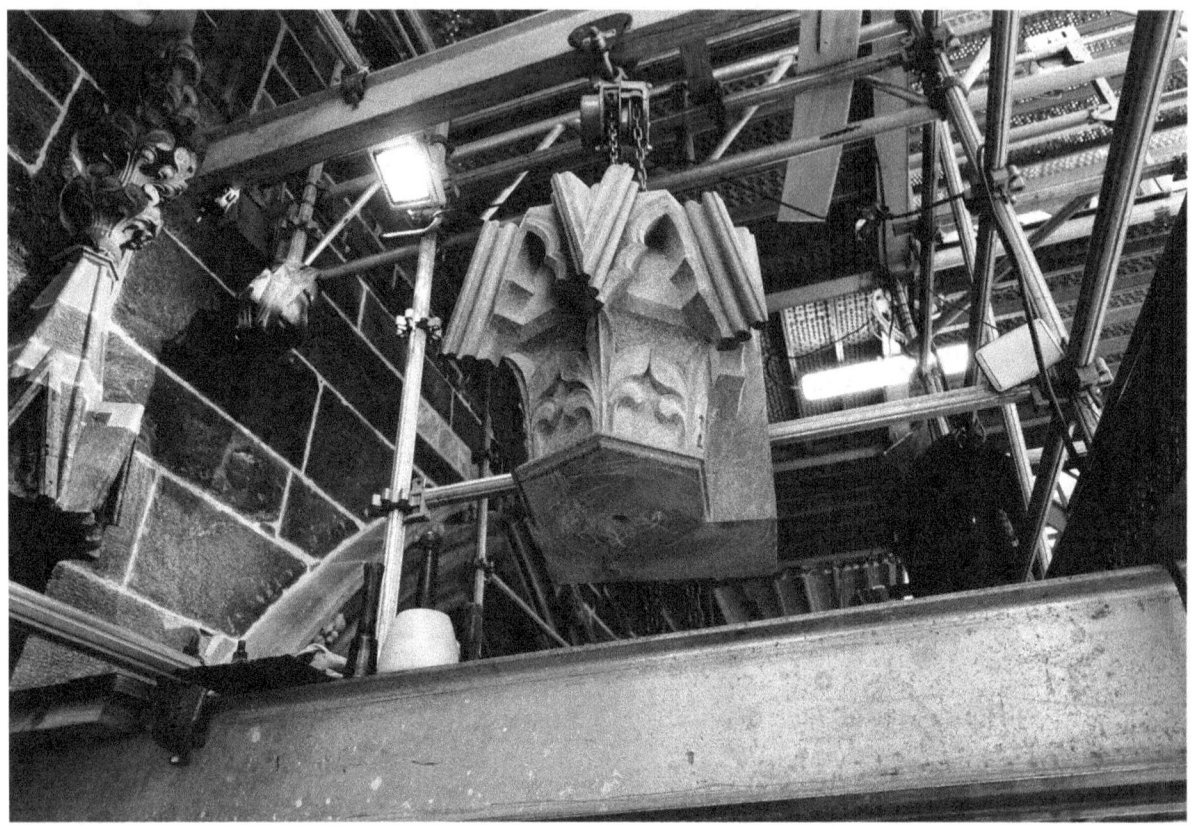

Stavanger domkirke, east façade; a heavy newly carved piece being installed using beams and various lifting equipment

In the case of the Domkirke, it helps that remnants of the old carvings direct the copies I make; in other words, less time is needed to reimagine its original forms.

2. *What happens if you make a mistake?*

The answer depends on the context. Often, just by the nature of working so closely to a piece of stone, an error or a slip of a chisel is blown way out of proportion. Of course, if a nose falls off a face, then it's a big deal, but for the most part the mistake is only as big as the chisel we use. Often when it matters the most, we are down to smaller and smaller chisels and so likewise the potential for a mistake is lessened. When I carve, I do keep in mind the possibility of something going wrong and occasionally think through worst-case scenarios, but I try to keep my focus on the desired outcome.

These are life lessons I learned from playing hours and hours of backgammon with my friend and fellow craftsperson George Murphy – a game that requires you to consider worst-case scenarios if you have any chance of properly calculating your next move, avoiding unnecessary risk and winning in the long run. Practically speaking, there are ways to alter the design slightly so that an error is minimised.

3. *How did you get into it?*

The answer to this is often disappointing for the question-asker because I can see that many people romanticize the craft. I do not have a romantic story of growing up amongst master carvers, captured by the mystery of stone or being inspired by poems or novels that touched on the craft. It was just a practical opportunity that landed when I was looking for a simple direction in life: I took a college stone masonry program. As it turned out, working with stone was not as simple as I had initially thought. The multitude of ways a stone can be used, manipulated, or discovered is the basis of what attracted me to the profession, and I continue to be swept up by what my peers create. That part is not so disappointing.

But I often imagine there is a fourth question running through people's minds, one they are too polite to ask: In this age of uncertainty, with digital technologies, global capitalism, and all the mechanical tools that

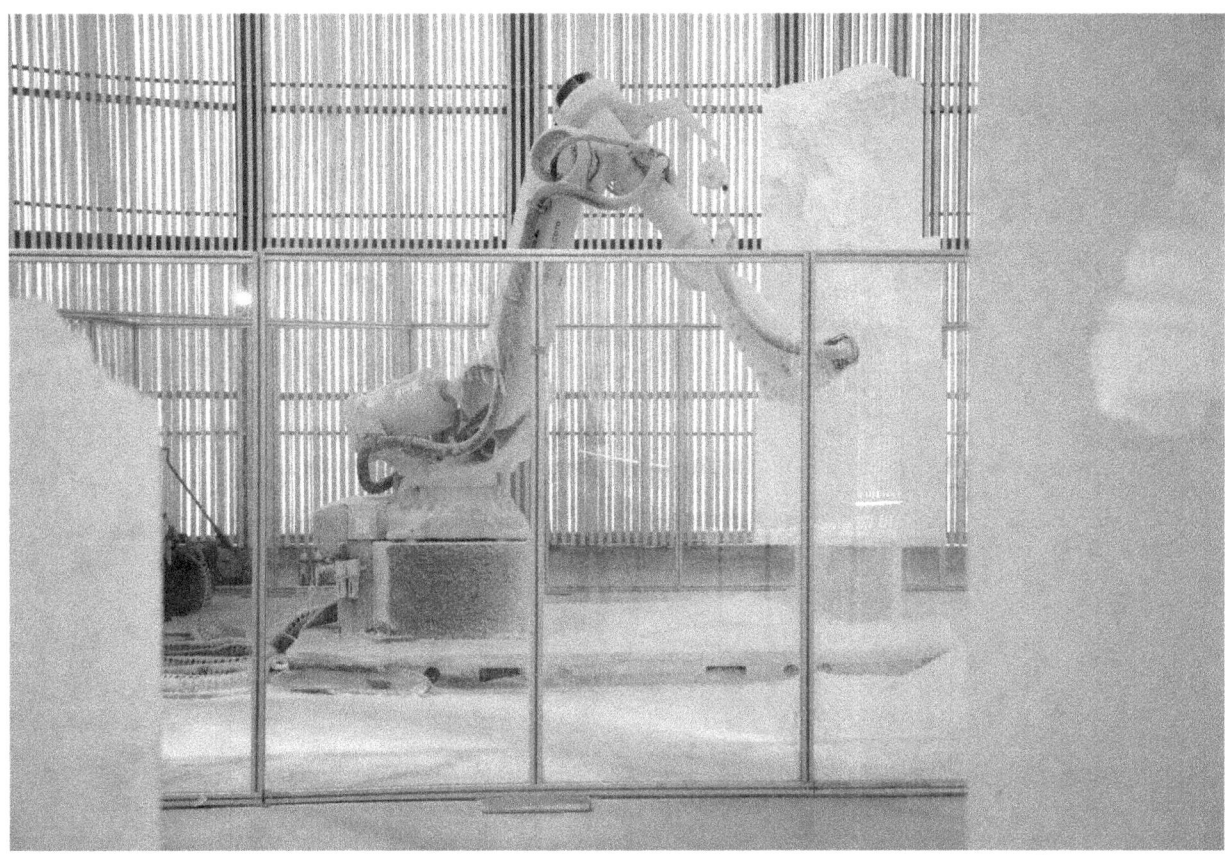

Robotic arm carving variations of Hellenic masterpiece Laocoön and His Sons. Photo credit: Sculpture Factory, Quayola.

are at our disposal, why all this effort and time to hand carve a piece of stone?

Reasons to reflect

The fourth question might be but the tip of the iceberg of philosophical questions that exist beneath the surface of my chosen craft. Removing material with a chisel and hammer is a very different experience from using conventional mechanical tools, and the textures they create are like the pencil marks you make when you draw; they are the lines you use to guide your work ahead. It is undoubtedly a slower method, but it brings into question why and for whom we carve.

For example, roughing out with a modern tool like a grinder - a electric hand tool with a fast-spinning diamond blade that slices into stone - removes and flattens stone with ease. What is lost is a complex feeling and connection one has with the stone; what is gained is noise, dust, and a different sense of pace. There is nothing inherently wrong with the grinder; I miss using it and find myself frustrated at times when I know a grinder could help me remove, in a matter of seconds, a hard quartz that's revealed itself in a stone.

I have read that painting can become a dialogue between the artist and their creation, giving meaning to what to keep, change and value. Just like a good conversation, collaboration is important to enable a harmonious outcome and to allow space for tensions that arise from differences in opinion. I find carving reflects these internal dialogues. Power tools can often expediate the process and though it may not necessarily diminish creativity I think it can limit opportunities for these dialogues to occur. Although efficiency is highly valued we should not narrow our perspective to valuing work on this single criteria. It raises the broader question of what role technology has in preserving cultural heritage. Restoring this cathedral is not only about preserving an important building, but as the planners of our project accurately gathered, it is also to preserve the traditional craft of carving.

It is futile to project or predict future outcomes, but I cannot talk about my own vocation here without quickly acknowledging the technologies that are, or already have become, popular commercially in making sculptures such as CNC

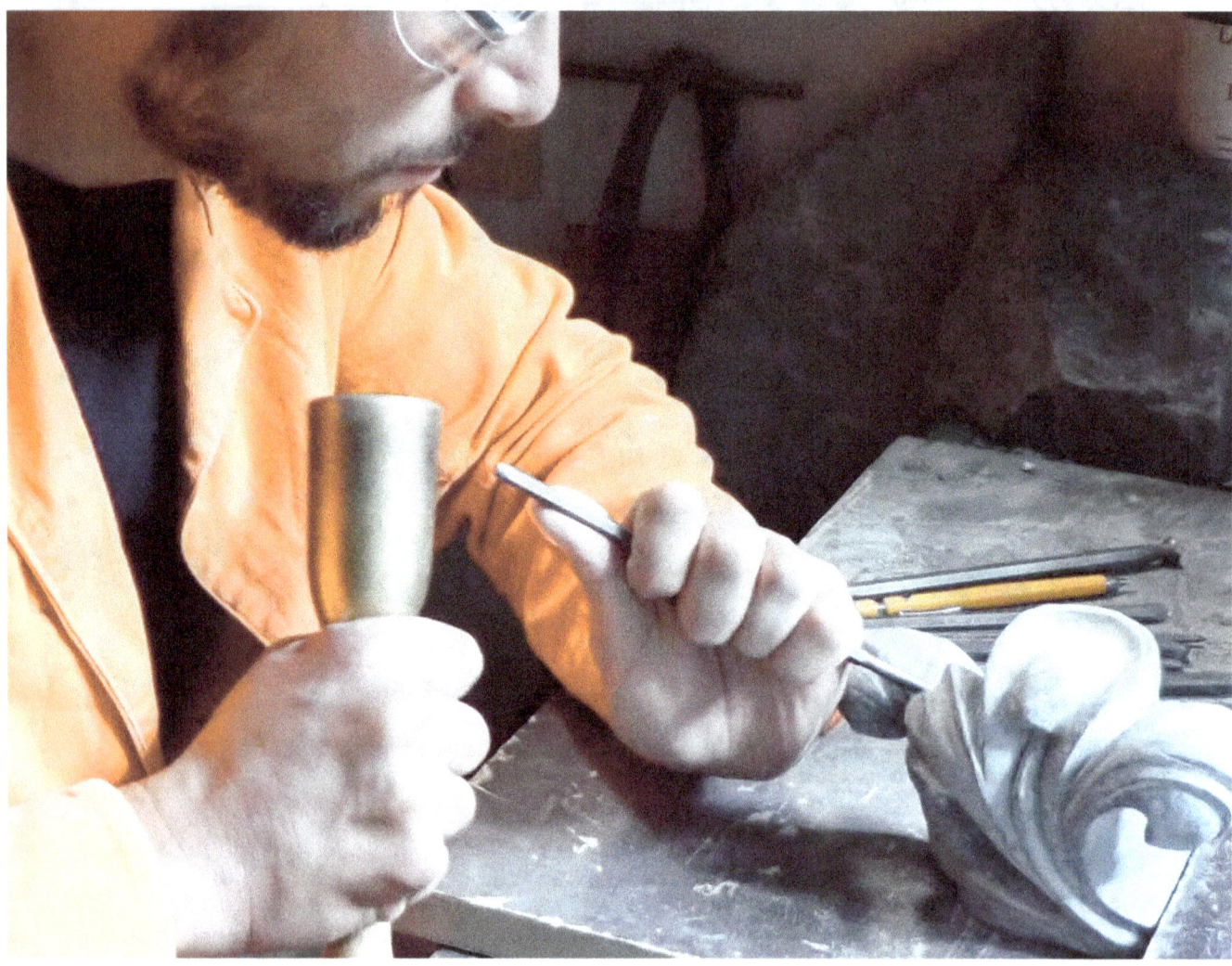

Akira at work

machines, 3D printing/scanning and AI. As I have heard said, soon we will have language, sound, and image combined in an app like ChatGPT to produce a video from a single written word or line. So, it isn't farfetched that the same accessible technologies can be combined with a 3D-modelling program and linked to a robotic arm to carve stone with very little effort or creative input from a human hand and mind. Three years ago, a robotic arm carved, non-stop in 250 hours, a copy of Canova's 'Cupid and Psyche' in Carrara marble with differences in surface texture so minimal one could not tell without seeing it up close.

It feels like our technological progress is moving faster than we as humans can fully comprehend and this requires us to slow down where we can, making space for reflection and consideration. Could our pursuit of speed and efficiency lead to the loss of autonomy and creativity? What responsibilities do we have for the future that we can take with us from the past?

In no way do I advocate an anti-technology point of view: new tools have a place and will expand the ways we create and communicate with our material world. They will even open the space for those who may not know how to carve to create works in stone--a scary, selfish thought for a carver who has dedicated almost half his life to the craft, but fantastic for the creative discourse when all walks of life are given an array of skills at their fingertips. I am but one person in a very small niche of craftspeople, part of a large group of other professions facing the same existential questions.

I have little doubt that there will always be some interest in the human touch. Such interest may diminish, perhaps as the necessity of that human touch becomes more distant. There is no way to determine objectively what is better. If we don't know who created the sculpture or how it was created, would we care? It can be argued that modern technology has led to a loss of both authenticity and a connection to the world around us. While this question needs further exploration and nuance, I am concerned that there are things which are lost when we introduce technology without critical thinking.

Instead of being swept up by technological progress, our approach to the Stavanger Domkirke has given us the time to understand our present position and the implications technology may have for the future of the craft. Equally, rather than blindly romanticizing the past we can extract the values that are relevant to us as humans today. People often comment, when they find out what I do, that I am the only person they have ever met engaged in what 'must be a dying trade'. A friend reminded me that death is what differentiates humans from AI, and that the Ancient Greeks knew the gods envied our mortality because it profoundly transformed our experience and understanding of the world. Dying isn't necessarily just about loss but provides us with a reason to reflect on what was, what is and what still might be – as long as one isn't dead entirely.

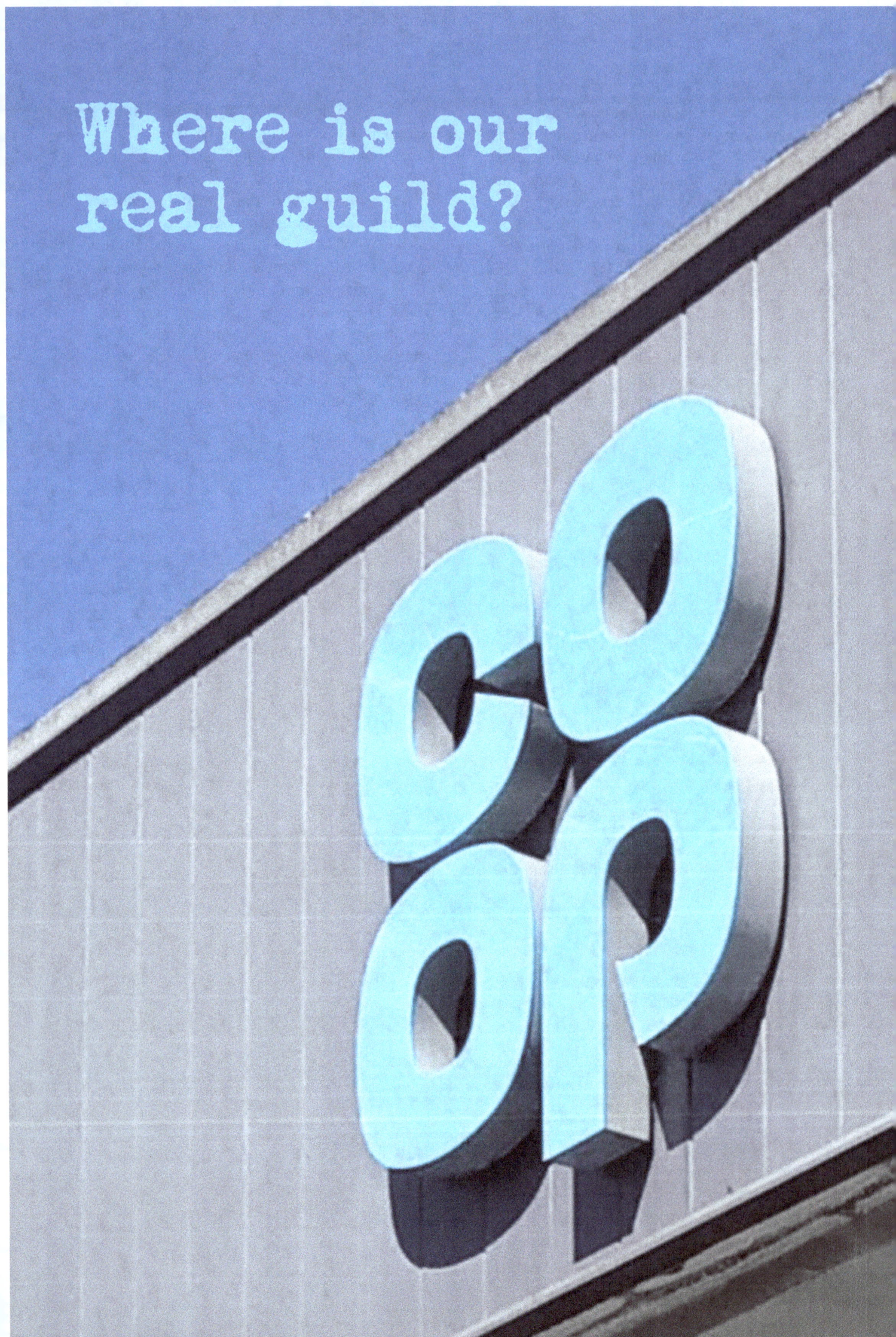

Π9 PROVOCATION 9

Carvers, co-operativism and the guild ideal
by Charles Tomlinson

Deep down in the heart of humanity there has always been the instinct for expression in line, form, and colour, the elaboration of which reveals the evolution of the mind behind it all. A sharpened flint and an unformed rock satisfied the needs of the prehistoric precursors of human society seeking to record the aspirations of their day. The rugged cave became the picture gallery of these early people, and on the walls we see to this day, in simple strokes and colours crude, figures of humans and animals that were ever in daily conflict in the struggle for existence. These stone scratchings marking the dawn of humanity's intelligence are as much works of art as are the graceful temples of ancient Rome and Greece and the magnificent cathedrals of the glorious Gothic world.

The highest art has historically been in the cause of religion — religion in its truest meaning, that is the binding of humankind to something higher than oneself. The grand edifices in marble left to us from ancient Babylon and Egypt, Greece and Rome, are all monuments of this fact. Still more eloquent evidence is the wonderful wealth of painted Christs and Madonnas, sung chants and hymns, and especially the wood and stone of the cathedrals and abbeys of the Middle Ages. In religion art is a kind of worship — or rather *worthship* as the word was originally known — the adoration or a reverence for something worthy, and all through this *worthship* the underlying principle was to serve the Common Good, whether viewed from the standpoint of the artist or the work of art itself. The artist, the artisan, was a pioneer in social advancement, and through art humankind could see the heights they had to climb before they could reach something more perfect.

Of course, there are diversities of gifts in art, but there is always the same spirit. We can talk of the art of the painter and the carver, of the musician and the singer, of the prophet and the poet, but their mission is always the same — to point the way to something more perfect.

Contray to a common assumption, history shows that co-operation in art is the vital force that leads to that goal. Art can no more live by and for itself than can an individual human being. It is as communal as is humankind, and no period shows this to a greater degree than the Middle Ages, a time when art and co-operation reached an ideal degree of partnership in the artisan guilds. The guilds were co-operatives and flourished throughout Europe. Whether sacred or secular, their foundation was based on mutual aid and social service. Amongst the greatest of the guild movements at that time were the guilds of stonecarvers and masons, corporations of artists in stone who gave the best of their craftsmanship wherever and whenever a church or cathedral had to be built. It was to the collaboration of these mediaeval workers working in co-operation and in co-operatives that we owe the great masterpieces of ecclesiastical architecture in Europe. The masons who worked on the grand cathedrals and the fine abbeys and minsters were not the egotistical individualists or the mere human machines of our own times, but people fired with the fervour of their art, who stamped each stone with the master-mark of their creativity.

Stonecarving tradition has it that the co-operative practice of the art of the stoneworker dates back to the old Roman Empire, or to the Pharaohs, or to the building of the Temple of Solomon. Perhaps even to the days of the Tower of Babel or the Ark of Noah, all passed down the generations, from master to apprentice. But we might wonder if this tradition survives to this day. It has been said that the industrialisation of the nineteenth century banished the tradition, and it is true that if the greatest period in the art of stonecarving was the Middle Ages, when the masters and apprentices of the craft-guilds held their labour to be sacred, the nineteenth century, saw the artisan turned into a slave to machinery. After that, the hands and brain the craftsman were no longer called upon to make 'a thing of beauty and a joy for ever' from a shapeless mass of material as a service of the people. Instead, the crafted object became a mechanical concoction, built up from standardised parts, so that the once-skilled shoemaker was divided into a creature of many parts, one to make the uppers, another to fix them to the sole, and so on. From that point onwards the machine became the master of things and the artisan suffered in body and soul under the domination of the Frankenstein of his own creation. This was the age of mechanised industrial competition, and its only beneficiaries were the idle Capitalist class who profited from other people's labour.

Competition is truly death — the death of all the highest motives in man. It is stagnation and the annihilation of the soul. The kind of co-operation to be found in the guild is life — the preservation of the human spirit and with it the preservation and expansion of human ideals. Co-operation, with its vital principle of 'Each for all, and all for each,' is the practical means to progress to that end. Art and co-operativism — one is an aesthetic ideal, the other an ethical one — are each part of one great body, and, as Tennyson has it,

> Like a piece of art,
> All toil should be co-operant to an end.

Well said, but where is our guild?

George Frederic Watts
Frederick Tennyson (plaster)
Watts Gallery, Guildford
c.1903

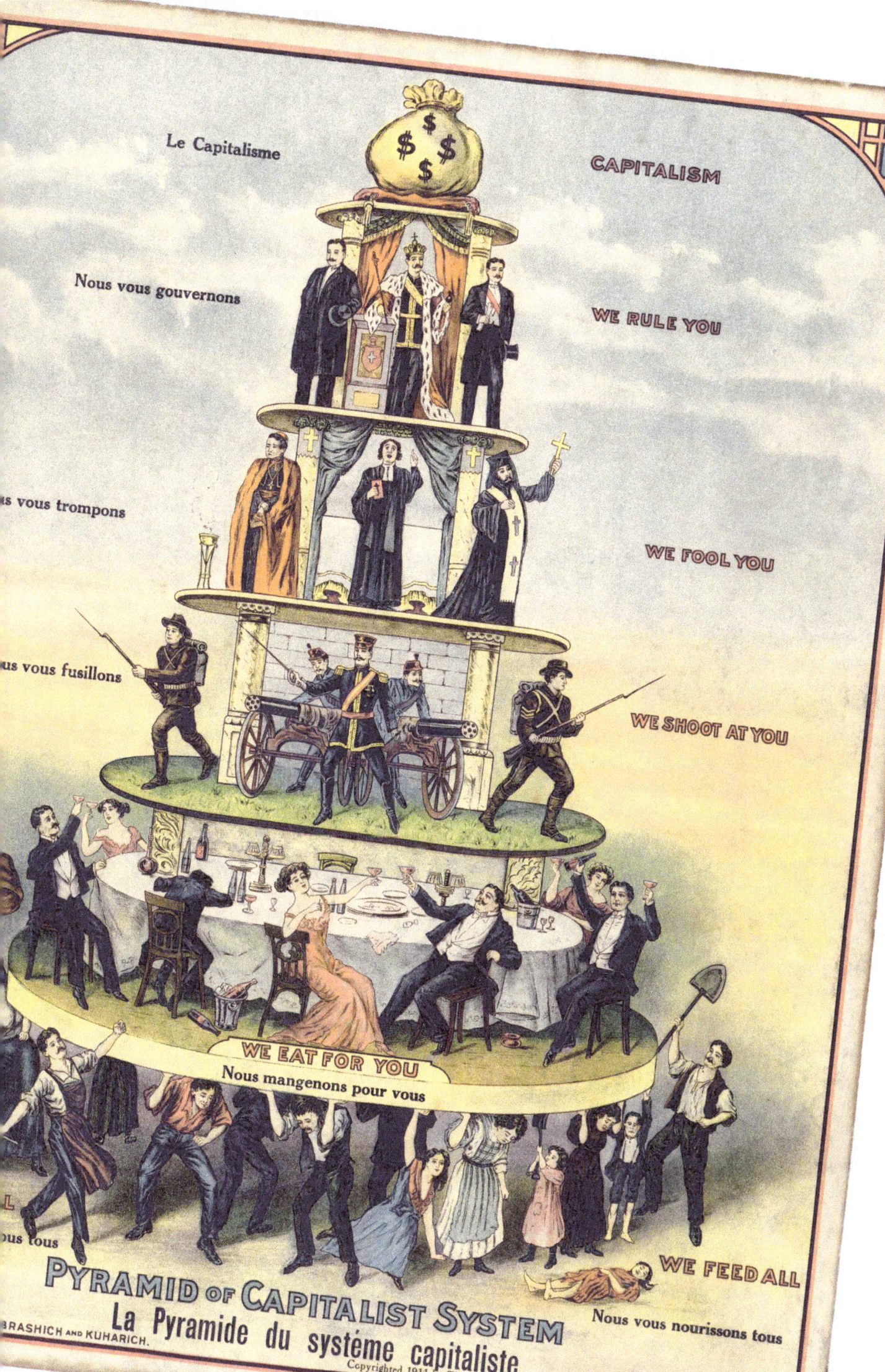

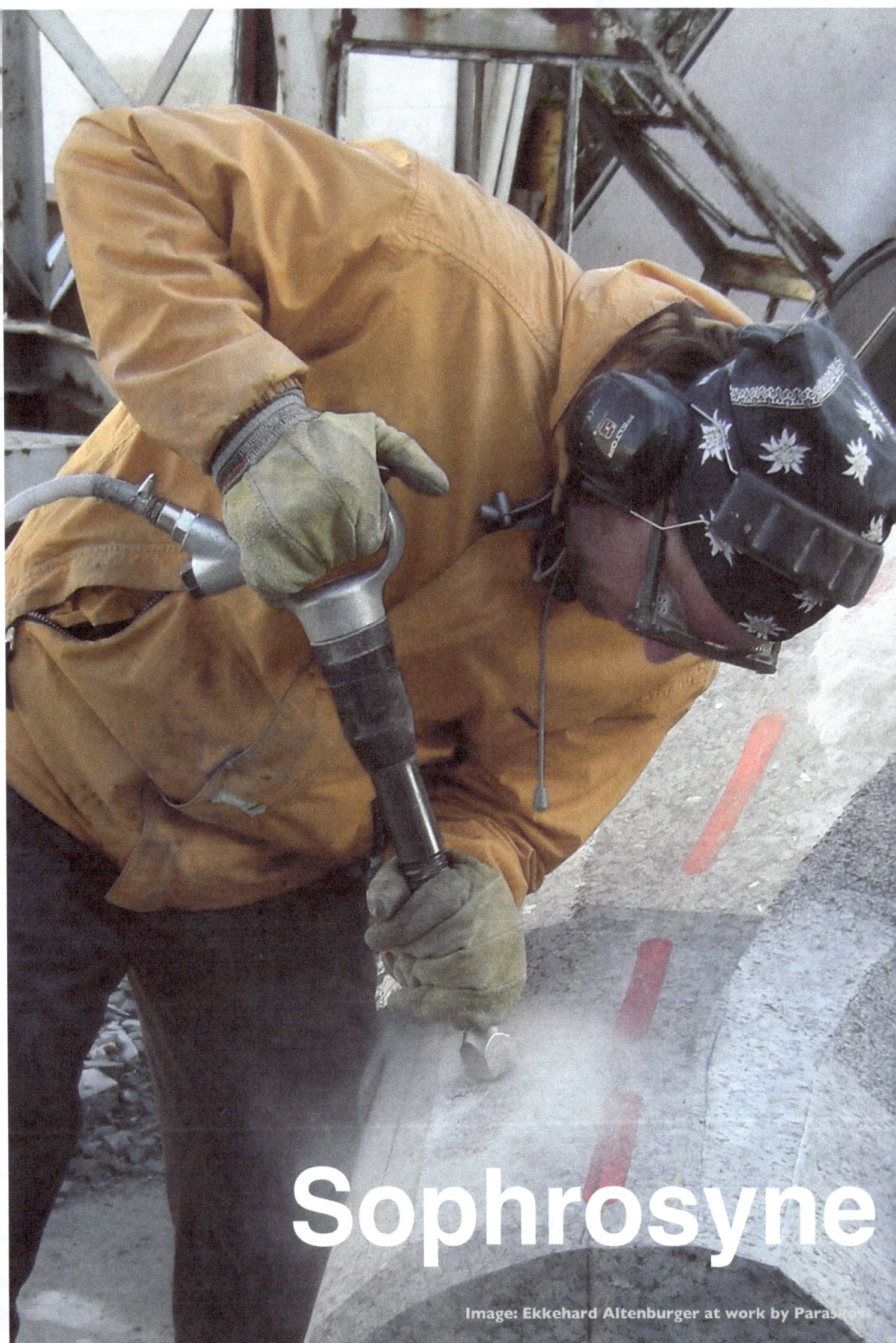

Sophrosyne

Image: Ekkehard Altenburger at work by Parasitos

PROVOCATION X

Profile: Ekkehard Altenburger
by Michael Paraskos

On 4 December 2009 I stood outside the studio of the artist Ekkehard Altenburger in Deptford, south London, on a visit to see the progress of a new sculpture he was creating for the town of Harlow in Essex.

At the time I was employed by the Harlow Art Trust to commission works of public art from artists like Ekkehard, and with me on that bitterly cold day was the chairman and secretary of the Harlow Arts Trust, Julian Rea and Kelly Lean, as well as William Moen, an idealistic property developer who was financing the whole project. I call Moen idealistic because he was not only interested in building new houses to sell for a profit, but wanted the people who lived in his houses to form a vibrant community. In this Moen followed in the footsteps of the original creator of Harlow, Frederick Gibberd, who also believed that having works of public art set amongst the homes and shops of Harlow helped foster a sense of community. It was this vision in Gibberd that resulted in Harlow having one of the largest collections of public sculpture, for a town its size, anywhere in Britain. It was also this vision, now in the hands of Moen, that meant I had to brave the December cold to see how Ekkehard's sculpture was coming along.

It was not a forgone conclusion that Ekkehard would win the commission for the new sculpture. As a registered charity, the Harlow Art Trust was bound by a legal requirement from the Charity Commission to follow strict rules when commissioning goods and services, even when that meant works of art. Consequently a long process had begun over a year earlier, which saw the Art Trust create a committee to oversee the commission, employ me as the Project Officer and advertise for interested artists to submit their ideas. We received over 150 proposals but these were reduced down to a shortlist of six candidates. Those candidates were asked to develop their proposals into fully-costed plans and invited to visit Harlow to present their ideas to the committee in person. Ekkehard was one of the invited artists.

What is remarkable is that almost straight away Ekkehard was the strongest candidate. It was a feeling shared by everyone on that committee after hearing his presentation, based partly on the look of the sculpture Ekkehard was proposing and on his approach to creating art.

Ekkehard intended to use an unusual stone, a hard granite from quarries in Norway, that would be shaped and then polished. This would be placed on a brightly coloured blue plinth, creating a vibrant contrast between the curving natural stone and the blue square platform on which it stood. It was a feature we noted in Ekkehard's earlier work. In images he showed us of public sculptures like 'Twisted Column' (2005: Queen Elizabeth Hospital, Gateshead) and 'Dopplereffect' (2007: Chelsea and Westminster Hospital, London) we saw the pairing of Estremoz marble, a pure white stone much-loved by the ancient Romans, with bright orange polymer paints in ways that were, to put it simply, visually exciting. Of course Ekkehard's proposed sculpture for Harlow looked very different to these, but it was clearly related to them, and it was the similarities and differences we saw between these works that appealed to us. We realised that through commissions like those in Gateshead and London, and now in Harlow, Ekkehard was creating a body of work that was evolving over time, drawing on past experiences to express new ideas. This approach was also emphasised by Ekkehard's written submission in which he quoted the French artist Henri Matisse: 'Making art is a bit like gardening: some things develop, some things die off and only a few

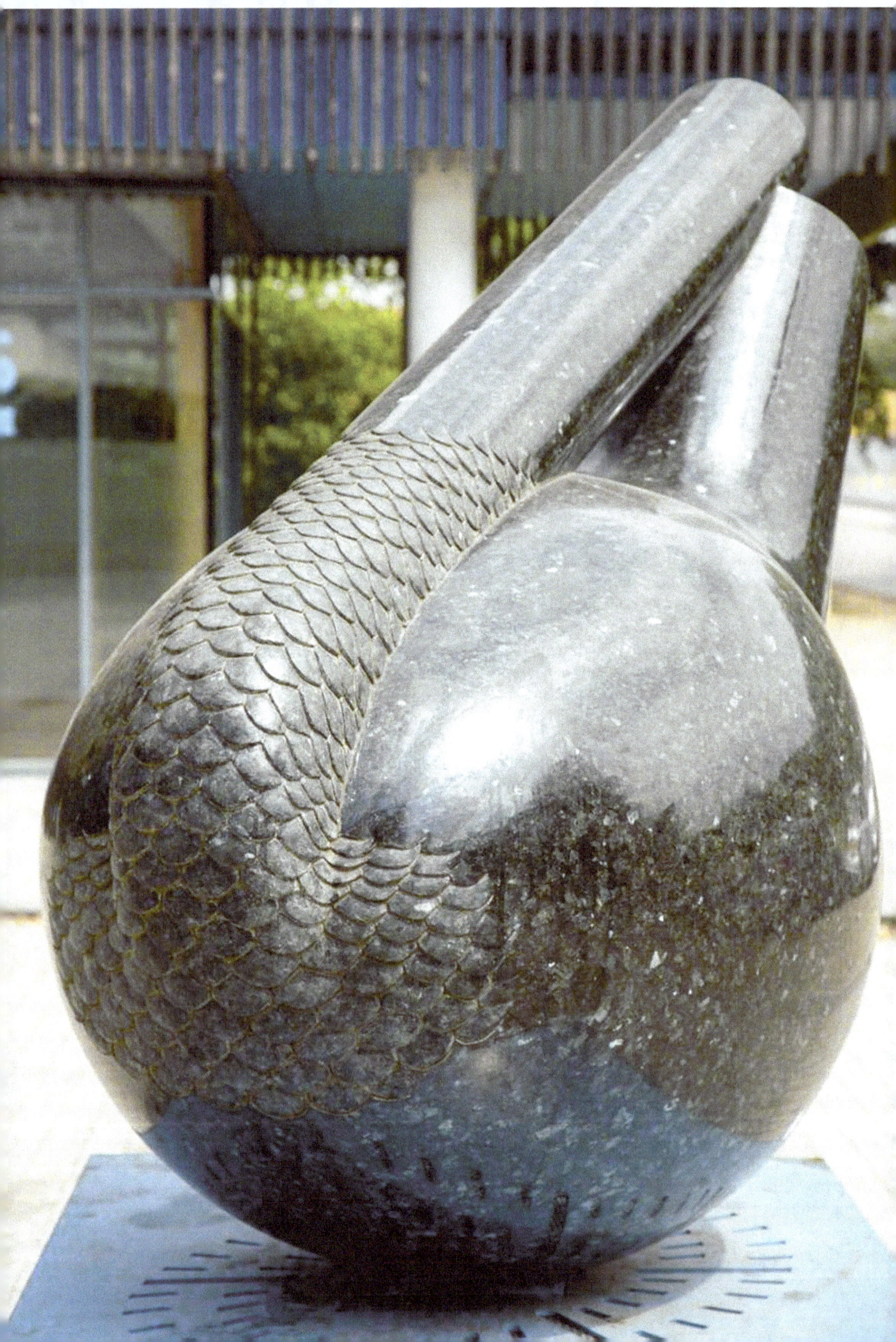

things will bear fruit.'

Ekkehard's attitude was in contrast to some of the other artists who had submitted proposals, who seemed determined to work to tried-and-tested formulas. Far too often there is a fundamental difference between gallery artists, who explore materials and ideas through art, and public sculpture artists, some of whom believe their role is simply to decorate a public space with formulaic work. Nothing illustrated this difference more clearly to the committee than Ekkehard's working method. While one of the shortlisted artists admitted he would not be making his proposed sculpture himself — instead a computer would do the carving for him in China — Ekkehard assured us that he would be carving the sculpture with his own hands. This fact swayed the committee firmly in his favour.

In his training Ekkehard differs from most sculptors today in that he began his sculpting career not in an art school but as an apprentice on the medieval cathedral of Schwabisch Gmuend, near Stuttgart. It was after learning the traditional skills of a stone carver that Ekkehard went on to study at art school, first at the Hochschule für Künste Bremen, and then at Edinburgh College of Art and Chelsea College of Art. This does not mean he is hostile to the use of new technology in his work, but it does explain where his respect for the stone he is using comes from and his moral commitment to take responsibility for the making process, whether he is using computer-guided machinery or a traditional hammer and chisel. We could say that he retains an almost medieval relationship to the stone he is working, even when he is using new technology. Because of this he remains a worker of stone rather than a maker of images in stone, and when it came to the commission at Harlow the committee wanted a worker of stone.

By the time of our visit to Ekkehard's studio in London in December 2009 the carving of the stone had progressed so that we could see the rough outline of the sculpture that would eventually become 'Sophrosyne'. Named after the ancient Greek goddess of moderation, balance and harmony, the work seems to evoke those virtues in the way it almost pivots on the base. Of course these qualities are expressed using an abstract sculptural language, but the sculpture does bring to mind figurative images, with some suggesting it is almost like a beautiful swan, with the long neck covered in scale-like carvings that could be read as stylised feathers. For others it evokes the perfect form of an ancient Greek urn, perhaps as a link back to the source of its title in ancient Greek mythology. But in reality it is a sculpture that elides numerous contrasts. It is abstract but almost figurative, it is made from natural stone bit this is set against the man-made plinth, it is formed from polished granite but this set against the unpolished scales, and it has a bulbous body but this is set against the swan-like neck. With each contrast and combination Ekkehard seeks to show a creative balance between the tension of difference and the harmony of integration that is at the heart of all great art, a feature Herbert Read also noted in relation to Henry Moore, calling it the 'dynamic tension' in his work.

Looking at the photographs we took on that December day when we visited Ekkehard's studio I am reminded of just how cold it was. Ekkehard worked outdoors in the only space that could accommodate something as large as a public sculpture. But I am also reminded of the excitement we all felt at seeing our sculpture for the first time. It was unfinished and there was still a long way to go before it was installed in Harlow the following summer, but we could see we had made the right choice in selecting Ekkehard for the commission. I remember too the excitement when Ekkehard charged up a noisy pneumatic chisel and began to show us his working method, taking lumps of stone from the block with the ease of a hot knife cutting through butter, but with as much care as a surgeon working in an operating theatre. It was a foretaste of the unveiling of the sculpture in New Hall in Harlow in the summer of 2010, where it has remained ever since, acting as Moen had hoped as a focal point for the identity of a new community.

The editor would like to thank the contributors for their time and labour in helping to put this publication together. This publication might be a small thing, but as Richard Demarco once said to me, *all revolutions start as small things.*